Equity in
School–Parent
Partnerships

Equity in School–Parent Partnerships

Cultivating Community and Family Trust in Culturally Diverse Classrooms

Socorro G. Herrera
Lisa Porter
Katherine Barko-Alva

Foreword by Luciana C. de Oliveira

TEACHERS COLLEGE PRESS

TEACHERS COLLEGE | COLUMBIA UNIVERSITY
NEW YORK AND LONDON

Published by Teachers College Press,® 1234 Amsterdam Avenue, New York, NY 10027

Library of Congress Cataloging-in-Publication Data

Names: Herrera, Socorro Guadalupe, author. | Porter, Lisa, author. | Barko-Alva, Katherine, author.
Title: Equity in school-parent partnerships : cultivating community and family trust in culturally diverse classrooms / Socorro G. Herrera, Lisa Porter, Katherine Barko-Alva.
Description: New York : Teachers College Press, 2020. | Includes bibliographical references and index.
Identifiers: LCCN 2020001855 (print) | LCCN 2020001856 (ebook) | ISBN 9780807763780 (paperback) | ISBN 9780807763797 (hardcover) | ISBN 9780807778517 (ebook)
Subjects: LCSH: Education—Parent participation—United States. | Community and school—United States. | Linguistic minorities—Education—United States. | Language and education—United States. | Culturally relevant pedagogy—United States. | English language—Study and teaching—Foreign speakers.
Classification: LCC LB1048.5 .H47 2020 (print) | LCC LB1048.5 (ebook) | DDC 371.19/2—dc23
LC record available at https://lccn.loc.gov/2020001855
LC ebook record available at https://lccn.loc.gov/2020001856

ISBN 978-0-8077-6378-0 (paper)
ISBN 978-0-8077-6379-7 (hardcover)
ISBN 978-0-8077-7851-7 (ebook)

Printed on acid-free paper
Manufactured in the United States of America

With love and respect for Gilberto Herrera and Esther Jaquez Herrera,
mis padres, who taught me to love and parent my four
beautiful children: Dawn, Kevin, Jesse, and Isamari.
—Socorro Herrera

To my amazing husband who has always been willing to take the road
less traveled; my mother who exemplifies courage, compassion, and
humility; my father who has instilled the joy of learning; and my three
incredible children who teach me every day about love and hope.
—Lisa Porter

To my parents, sistercita, mamá Erito, papá Alfonso, *and*
my kind husband. Your sacrifice, love, and entrega *know no bounds.*
Gracias a ustedes, *I have been able to travel this teaching and*
learning journey with confianza y compasión.
—Katherine Barko-Alva

Contents

Foreword

Working with parents in K–12 schools is one of the most important aspects of a teacher's work. Yet in my work with preservice and in-service teachers I have witnessed a general struggle in schools to engage parents in significant ways. Parental involvement and engagement go beyond parents attending school events and meetings. It is especially important to understand what real parental involvement and engagement is, especially for culturally and linguistically diverse (CLD) communities. In this era of fear and misinformation about immigration, it is paramount that administrators, teachers, school counselors, and all school personnel understand the experiences and knowledge that parents bring to schools. It is important to know that parental involvement also includes the many diverse ways parents participate in activities at home to ensure opportunities for success for their children.

The centrality of parental involvement and engagement in our field, Teaching English to Speakers of Other Languages (TESOL), has been well established in the research and practical literature. Despite the value placed on this topic, there are few resources educators can turn to that informs their skills to engage parents. This book by Socorro G. Herrera, Lisa Porter, and Katherine Barko-Alva is a necessary and welcome addition to the field. It addresses the questions "How can families feel respected, valued, listened to, and supported?" and "How can schools examine their paths of least resistance—practices that occur simply because they always have—and challenge their roles, responsibilities, and biases?" Rooted in both theory and practical applications, the authors use vignettes, discussion and reflection questions, visuals, and engagement activities embedded throughout the book to involve readers in the content and help them consider the important ideas, concepts, and notions put forth.

The authors start the book with a chapter focusing on challenging schools to examine the misconceptions they have about parental involvement and engagement and offer a review of parental engagement models, including their principles, contributions, and questions.

Chapter 2 explores the concepts of *languaging*, goes into language practices of immigrant families as they move into new communities and need to use their language resources to navigate new systems, and discusses communication needs of schools to better support parental involvement and engagement. Chapter 3 explores the concept of homework, focusing on fixed notions to re-conceptualize it. Grounded in a philosophy of *cariño*, the chapter provides educators with ways to incorporate CLD families' experiences and assets in the curriculum. Chapter 4 examines and challenges the concepts of family, school, and community and examines culturally responsive teaching principles and competencies. Challenging these concepts involves developing *conscientização*, as Paulo Freire puts it, or critical consciousness, the process of recognizing oppressive systems as the basis for sustainable transformation of these systems, as the authors highlight in the chapter. In Chapter 5, the authors describe specific instructional contexts in which many CLD students are placed: ESL and dual language classrooms. This chapter highlights the need to prioritize intercultural understandings and radical kinship as the basis for dual language programs to develop transformative engagement activities for families. Chapter 6 challenges educators to re-conceptualize and reconstruct their ideas and actions about racial and cultural issues. The final chapter, Chapter 7, develops the idea of a pedagogy of hope, using a school district as an example and emphasizing *assets* as important points of departure for working with families. The authors conclude the book with examples of how consciousness and courage combined can lead to collectively hope for CLD parental involvement and engagement.

Herrera, Porter, and Barko-Alva challenge us to assess our understandings and knowledge about working with CLD families and offer practical suggestions to re-examine assumptions. This is a must-have book for schools that serve CLD populations and teacher educators who prepare teachers for such work.

—Luciana C. de Oliveira,
Associate Dean for Academic Affairs and Professor,
Virginia Commonwealth University
Past President (2019–2020), TESOL International Association

Acknowledgments

The authors of this book would like to first and foremost thank the families, teachers, administrators, and districts that have allowed us to share their stories and visit their homes and facilities. The journey of writing a book involves synergistic collaboration not only between and among the authors of the book, but also with the brilliant minds that provide their time and energy throughout the process. We would like to thank Melissa Holmes for guiding and challenging us to dig a little deeper and explore a little further until the words flowed on the pages in ways that brought to life what we intended to say to the reader. Latania Marr worked diligently to explore research that laid hidden beyond the boundaries of our searches. Her questions, feedback, and contributions brought in new perspectives on families. As always Sheri Meredith's attention to detail helped to refine this book and get it to completion. Without our village this work would not have been possible. Finally, thank you to Sylvia Whitney Beitzel for her endless commitment to working with CLD families and her creative ideas on authentic engagement.

Introduction

Preparing this book has been a commitment to the ideal we hold for a future where parental engagement is re-envisioned within our communities and schools. Each of us as faculty, teachers, community activists, and mothers look to a future filled with hope for opening up spaces where voices, experiences, and knowledge are valued equally. Our current U.S. political climate has left many culturally and linguistically diverse (CLD) families feeling marginalized both inside and outside the walls of schools. Feelings of inferiority, exclusion, and fear are constants as they navigate the barrage of negative commentary and quick-fire policies surrounding immigration fostered under the Trump administration. Fear is not limited to undocumented families and students; it affects all marginalized families and students who are CLD.

Public schools often have been described as a microcosm of society. The political, social, and economic happenings within a nation impact the climate of local schools. The trust that is required to establish reciprocal and engaged relationships between schools and families is more critical now than ever. The stakes are high, and beyond feeling alienated from the daily happenings within schools, parents now are trying to decipher if schools are safe at all. Regardless of our sociopolitical views, this socioemotional context creates a challenging reality for the mutual engagement of parents and educators. It bears asking the question, again, at the most fundamental level: What does it mean to engage a parent/caregiver/family in an era of fear?

Thinking about societal issues is imperative when attempting to strengthen relations and build trust between families and schools. Often, struggles that families face are part of a greater societal issue. In Western societies, however, we tend to place responsibility and blame exclusively on individuals without looking at the situation from a more systematic lens. Social systems, such as transportation, housing, employment, education, and politics affect our lives in very direct ways. Yet, when examining behaviors, tendencies, or responses of individuals or families, these systems are seldom factored into the equation. If people are struggling with addiction, society tells them to "beat it" without recognizing the lack of treatment facilities across the country for those in crisis. When someone is obese, society blames the person for overeating rather than addressing the failing U.S. health system or the extremely low prices of processed foods made from government-subsidized products. Similarly, single mothers frequently are looked down on for seeking government assistance, in place of having discussions about how it is more affordable for such mothers to do so than to attempt securing child care on today's minimum wage.

Individualizing social issues as personal problems is a common occurrence inside public schools as well. If a child is perpetually late to school, the family tends to receive blame, usually without school officials knowing the circumstances. If a child's parent never comes to school conferences or returns phone calls, opinions about his or her commitment tend to form. When a child returns to school with incomplete homework, it is assumed the child was negligent or no one in the family was able to help, rather than exploring the exclusionary practices of homework.

The aim of this book is to help us recognize that relationships are never 50/50 and that engagement does not equate to participation at school functions. Rather, engagement is a collective promise built on trust that goes beyond learning gains and attendance and instead is about caring for one another without judgment or expectation. Skeptics of this book may argue that such rhetoric has no substance and offers little assistance to schools committed to improving family and community engagement. In the chapters to come, we will challenge this perspective by illustrating how engagement models, procedures, innovative projects, and collaborative school events will not produce lasting results without our first establishing a mindset that is rooted in *agradecimiento* (gratitude) and humility. How can families feel respected, valued, listened to, and supported? How can schools examine their paths of least resistance—practices that occur simply because they always have—and challenge their roles, responsibilities, and biases? This book will provide practical steps educators can take toward building strong relationships with the families and communities of their students.

This book examines fossilized practices within today's educational system that can potentially marginalize and devalue the contributions and cultural biographies of families, particularly CLD families. Based on the research and K–12 teaching experience of three educators who currently work with families, teachers, and administrators in the field, this book creates opportunities for reflection and provides suggestions for school communities seeking to re-envision the meaning of parental involvement and engagement, as well as perspectives and tools to better prepare our teaching and leadership candidates. Supported by educational and sociological theory, each chapter addresses contemporary issues, such as the "absent" parent, homework, vulnerable populations, limitations of current school-based family programs, and pedagogies of hope. Readers will find vignettes, discussion questions, visuals, and engagement activities embedded throughout the book to serve as thought-provoking and useful resources.

Following is an introduction to the chapters. Each chapter asks readers to reflect on their current parental engagement model or program. How does it currently set the stage to *engage, respect,* and *accept* all parents/caregivers, regardless of their background/history? Only when we begin to ask difficult questions will our work in schools support us to maximize the assets of all parties involved.

Chapter 1, "Questioning Limiting Visions: Reconceptualizing Engagement Possibilities," prepares the reader to engage in a journey of discovery to unpack what has been and what currently exists with parent involvement and engagement, and to explore new possibilities. This chapter addresses obstacles beyond language acquisition that CLD families face, especially hegemonic practices and systematic barriers commonly found in public schooling. This chapter emphasizes key U.S. Supreme Court cases that address students' language rights and educational access. We analyze limitations of top-down approaches to educational reform and their impact on CLD families. We also provide an overview of models, frameworks, and philosophies that currently guide school-centric parent engagement efforts. We suggest instead an asset-based approach to understanding and working with families. In this chapter, we also summarize the work of scholars and researchers who informed our own ideas of what it means to reimagine possibilities for school–parent/caregiver relationships.

Chapter 2, "They Just Don't Show Up," focuses on hegemonic usages of language and provides examples of how language in public schools creates unequal power structures that alienate CLD families. The chapter begins by problematizing longstanding instructional practices and perceptions of the "absent parent." Through examples of school-centric dichotomous language often used when examining parent responsibilities, the chapter explores how families are often shamed and blamed for situations that are the result of systematic inequalities rather than individual deficiencies. The chapter examines common perceptions of families who don't participate in school functions and supports a paradigm shift of what it truly means to "show up" in the lives of children in their educational journey. The chapter concludes with intrinsic as well as extrinsic steps toward recognizing entrenched ways of seeing, in order to begin to create more inclusive spaces.

Chapter 3, "Burying Fossilized Practices: Disrupting *los Deberes* (Homework)," highlights fossilized practices within public education, focusing specifically on homework. By examining the meaning, practices, and historical shifts of homework, we explore alternative ways of approaching homework, or *los deberes*. Analyzing the meaning of *los deberes* as an action-based concept, we urge educators to rethink their usage of homework to better connect with families and their interests, histories, and skillsets, or *manualidades*. This begins with teachers cultivating an authentic *cariño* (loving care) for the families they serve in order to reconceptualize their classroom ecology and transform pedagogical practices to foster relations with CLD families.

Chapter 4, "Broadening Conceptions of Community in Engagement," problematizes fixed notions of home, school, and community and the impact these notions have on relationships with CLD families. We continue by exploring the meaning of parental engagement and providing examples of typical school-based attempts to connect the school with CLD families as well as the broader community (e.g., home visits, business donation appeals). We argue that these practices, although important, are points in time rather than ongoing exchanges. Further, they all are school-led initiatives. As part of this chapter, we examine the need to involve all caregivers (e.g., neighbors, mentors, leaders within community) in our conception of parental engagement, and the impact this can have on student learning. Broadening the meaning of community and establishing ongoing exchanges provides students with cultural context for their language learning and motivates them to serve as change agents within their communities. Educators are encouraged to refrain from always being the drivers of community initiatives and to support parent-led organizing whenever possible.

Chapter 5, "Planting on Fertile Ground: ESL/Dual Language Programs and Parental Engagement," seeks to uncover and examine barriers that alienate parents or prevent their involvement in English as a second language (ESL) and dual language (DL) programs. The chapter highlights how school spaces are shared but never neutral and how priority often is given to parents who are white, have access to financial resources, and are fluent in English. The chapter analyzes how such practices create divided spaces and closed school cultures, causing parents to feel alienated and even excluded. We urge readers to examine how such feelings might be compounded by institutional policies intended to protect and support. We conclude this chapter with practical guidelines that can lead to a cultural shift in the school ecology, from *simplemente ¡Buenos días!¿Cómo está?* (simply Good morning! How are you?), to piloted parental engagement ideas that embrace equitable practices. Suggestions are designed for school communities to replicate or use as templates based on individual program needs. Ideas for parent groups on how to organize and advocate are also provided.

Chapter 6, "Projecting Our Socialization No Longer: *Pobrecitos Hijos y Padres* (Pity for Poor Children and Parents)," begins by providing a framework to support exploration of our readiness to accommodate the assets and needs of CLD students and families. The chapter also explores the term *pobrecito,* and we warn readers of the inclination to either blame or pity. We emphasize the necessity of *cariño* as an ethic that reflects respect, collaboration, commitment, and compatibility rather than judgement. This chapter is written for the naysayers who argue that ideas in this book are unrealistic, or for those in the teaching profession who claim, "It is not my job to be a social worker." We acknowledge these sentiments but argue that understanding biographies of children and their families is an integral component to achieving learning outcomes and modeling collaboration that allows students, families, and educators to support one another.

Chapter 7, "Furthering the Pedagogy of Hope," builds on the works of Paulo Freire. Like all things, when something is broken, you don't keep using it. Yet when it comes to parental engagement among CLD parents, schools continue to use fossilized practices that alienate parents from the very programs that purport to support language instruction and cultural inclusivity. Contrary to common perception, CLD parents are eager to be involved with their children's learning. And, despite feeling overwhelmed, educators have always been good at working between the lines. Hope does not die. This chapter demonstrates how the contents of this book can be used as a framework for a pedagogy of hope reliant on agency and advocacy.

Equity in School–Parent Partnerships

CHAPTER 1

Questioning Limiting Visions
Reconceptualizing Engagement Possibilities

Knowing is not enough; we must apply. Willing is not enough;
we must do.

—Johann Wolfgang von Goethe

Key Concepts: sociological imagination, relational trust, capital, funds
of knowledge, dialogue, cultural compatibility

INTRODUCTION

We begin this chapter by asking ourselves: Is our focus parental engagement, parental involvement, or authentic *cariño* (loving care), *confianza* (trust), and respect? Current literature can be confusing with
regard to which model or school/classroom activity is going to engage
parents in supporting the school to achieve the ultimate goal: increased
academic success for all students. Less frequently does the conversation in the literature ask: Who are the parents we serve, and what can
we learn from each to better meet the needs of the learner? Yet to plan
effective parental engagement activities, wouldn't it help if we knew
the community and parents/caregivers within our schools? What if we
worked in reverse order (backward mapped) when we thought about
parents? Then, instead of first pondering what parents need to know
to support their children, we would consider what we need to know
about the family to support our planning for instruction and engagement. Our subsequent efforts to plan school and classroom activities
would likely yield more equitable opportunities for all. Think about the
following scenarios.

Scenario 1:

Denise is a single mother with one daughter. She is a nurse at the local hospital. Denise understands the importance of being present to her daughter's needs. She makes sure she is only scheduled to work when her daughter is in school. Her boss is very flexible with her time and encourages her to attend all school events without penalty. She is then given the opportunity to make up the time. Denise's favorite time of the day is when she puts her daughter to bed and reads her favorite bedtime stories.

Scenario 2:

Angela and Jose moved to a rural community in the last year to follow their dream of obtaining a better education for their children. The move was (and continues to be) difficult. For the first half of the year, the family lived with a cousin who had moved to the midwestern rural community where they now live. Angela and Jose finally saved enough money for the family of six to move into a small house. Their children settled into the elementary, middle, and high school and now seem to be doing well. Their greatest challenge initially had been transporting their four children to three different schools. Jose works all night and Angela works all day. Juggling schedules is difficult, and the transportation eventually had to be turned over to their neighbor. Although this works most of the time, their neighbor also has other responsibilities. On days she cannot take them, the kids stay home and have to miss school.

Scenario 3:

Sam and Jackie have two kids. A few years ago, they decided that Jackie would not work and would instead stay home with their children to provide them with the same type of stability they both had as children. Jackie loves serving as room mother during the day, serving on the PTA board, and supporting the district on leading initiatives for new technology and gym equipment, as well as helping to pass new bonds to improve schools. Her children know she will be there before, during, and after school. Sam is happy in his job and financially stable enough to support Jackie in staying home for as long as she wants, without giving up any extras such as family vacations.

Think about the life choices that each of these parents has made to become involved/engaged. Do you see similar family stories within your own context? As you engage in reading this book, think about the parents you serve. How might their life trajectories impact their participation in our schools and classrooms? What do these three short scenarios say to us about the questions we should raise in our work with parents?

WITH THE BEST OF INTENTIONS, WE'VE FAILED TO ARRIVE

Our orchestration of the work we plan and deliver on a daily basis in our classrooms, schools, and districts is grounded on the premise that we are, in very intentional ways, guided by the learner and what's best for achieving his or her potential. The emotional well-being and academic success of our community of learners are part of our mission statements in schools and in our daily conversations. Without fail, research and literature (e.g., Bus, van Ijzendoorn, & Pellegrini, 1995; Hill & Taylor, 2004; Jeynes, 2003; Lopez, 2001b; Price-Mitchell, 2009; Wilder, 2014) have clearly found that central to the learner's emotional well-being and academic success—and to our teaching—is the need for strong parental involvement and engagement in school and classroom settings. Yet parental involvement and engagement have continued to function in mechanistic ways, with very prescriptive notions of a parent's role.

Watson and Bogotch (2015) remind us that the challenges often shared by teachers and administrators about involving or engaging parents, especially culturally and linguistically diverse (CLD) parents/caregivers are reflective of a system that neither questions nor disrupts normative constructions of the terms *parental involvement* and *parental engagement*. Instead, parent involvement and engagement are often guided by premises of how the parent/caregiver is to behave, discipline, and engage—that is, to parent. Unintentionally, caregivers and parents are stripped of what they know and can do for their child both in and out of school.

Historically, these guidelines, recommendations, and premises have been defined and driven through a monocultural lens, without consideration or reflection on the complexity of how "parent" is defined across culturally bound communities and homes. To understand how schools have come to define these terms for today's stakeholders, it is important to understand their beginnings. According to

Schlossman (1976), the origins of our current underpinnings of parent involvement date back to 1897, when the National Congress of Mothers was formed. Early on, the associations were formed to provide a forum for parents to have a say in their child's education. Those early associations had the power to make consequential decisions about curricula, teacher hiring and firing, and monitoring of how students were prepared for citizenship in the world (Prentice & Houston, 1975). Parent involvement in the 1930s shifted the way parents were involved in schools and began to resemble what it is today, with associations setting reform agendas, policies, frameworks, and models to accomplish the goal of involving parents in school.

A paradigm that seeks to educate and define for parents *what*, *how*, and *when* they are to be engaged and involved in their child's education now prevails (Epstein, 2001). From how many books to read (and for how long), to what play looks like from birth to preschool, to tips for everything from parenting a teenager to deciding the parameters of extracurricular commitments, schools endeavor to teach families what it means to parent. For immigrant families, this means redefining through a normative lens what it means to raise their children. More often than not, this lens is conceived through a narrow view guided by the dominant culture of this country, raising the question: Is there not anything we could learn from immigrant parents about engagement in today's schools? In this chapter we explore the questions: What is involvement? What is our intended purpose for espousing the need to have involved parents to ensure a learner's academic success?

Decades of research have continued to place CLD parents at the margins, blaming poverty, single-parent family status, and lack of education for their children not achieving academically at the same level as their white, monocultural, monolingual, English-speaking peers (Watson & Bogotch, 2015). What remains unquestioned within the institution we call "school" is how the power dynamics, language, and unquestioned definitions of engagement and involvement serve to write the narrative for what it means to create an equitable space for participation of all parents. This failure requires us to reexamine the narrow definition educators have of parental engagement and involvement.

Dismantling the Narrative

By design, schools continue to favor the discourse that values current definitions for parental engagement and involvement, discounting and undermining the powerful voices and lived experiences of CLD caregivers/families. Often the focus is on how often the parent reads with the child, attends school functions, or is involved with school events. LaRocque and colleagues (2011) state that administrators and other school educators disregard how limiting these current parameters for involvement can be for the family member that has, for example, an all-night shift at a beef packing plant, limited child-care services, and other life challenges not often faced by middle-class parents.

Reconceptualizing the parameters for parental involvement and letting go of perceiving parents through a social and cultural deficit lens will advance the role parents play in schools. Beginning this journey will require that educators let go of hierarchical relationships in which knowledge rests solely within schools. The reinventing of caregiver/family involvement and engagement begins with posing critical questions about how different languages and cultures are embodied and present within the ecologies of our schools. What boundaries exist? How in the box is our thinking about where parental partnerships fit into our work? Within this complexity there must be openness to cocreating new knowledge, engaging in open dialogue, and recognizing the multitude of stories we must seek and truly listen to if we are to understand the unique characteristics of the caregivers/families we serve. Without revisiting school and classroom cultures and definitions for engagement and involvement, we will be guided and driven by court cases and models that are left at the espoused—that is, talk without the action or application in practice.

Legalese: What Does It Mean in Practice?

Advocates for the rights of learners have long fought the battle to guarantee that the most basic of CLD students' educational rights be at the forefront. Court decisions detail the importance of working closely with families to ensure the native language is honored and used as an asset during instruction. Decisions further provide guidelines on the importance of informing parents/guardians on programming, educational rights, and their role in being present to evaluate the effectiveness of services provided for their children. Court cases serve as the fundamental beginning for creating a path that ensures an equitable space for CLD students to learn. Take time to consider how parental involvement has evolved over time, and how the cases and reforms summarized in Table 1.1 can be applied to your educational context.

Table 1.1. History of Family Engagement in the United States

From the Beginning	
National Congress of Mothers (1897)	• Formed because parents perceived significant separation between parent control and public schools. • Comprised of upper- and middle-class mothers who voiced their concerns to principals through petitions. • Studied school curriculum and growth of children. • Desired to inspire other parents to get involved in the education of their children.
First Parent Teacher Association (PTA) Meeting (1897)	• First meeting organized to study the social science research regarding child welfare in the home, at school, and in society.
PTA (1898)	• Became an incorporated national association and continued the work undertaken during the first meeting (child welfare in the home, at school, and in society). • Led by women reformers during this Progressive Era. • Helped influence the curriculum to value childrearing. • Furthered the goal to "Americanize newcomers to the country and to teach middle class parenting" (Davies, 1992, as cited in Hiatt-Michael, 2010, p. 254).

Supreme Court Cases

Causes:

• As school bureaucracy increased over the years, parents resorted to the courts in an attempt to lessen bureaucracy in public schools.
• Parents sought equality of educational opportunities for their children.

Cases	Implications for CLD Families	Implications for Families and Schools
Meyer v. Nebraska (1923)	• In 1919, the *Siman Act* passed in Nebraska and made it illegal for any private or public school to support foreign language instruction for students below the 8th grade. • The Supreme Court overturned this law, stating that it was unconstitutional for states to pass laws banning communities from implementing language classes outside regular school hours.	• Schools, districts, and families should work together on efforts toward implementing home language programs for EL populations. Program funding and evaluation should be ongoing.

Cases	Implications for CLD Families	Implications for Families and Schools
	• This case provided the foundation for bilingual education.	
Brown v. Board of Education of Topeka (1954)	• This case ruled that separate schools were not providing equal opportunities for Black and White children. It led to other desegregation cases across the country.	• Teachers, administrators, and families should understand the racial and cultural demographics of classrooms. CLD students should be represented in honors and advanced placement classes as well as international baccalaureate programs. Students' home language and English language proficiency should be mediated and celebrated in every classroom.
Lau v. Nichols (1974)	• This case promoted bilingual education for ELs so they benefit equally from public education. • The case ruled that "equal is not equitable"; language-minority students had access to neither the language of instruction (English) nor meaningful learning experiences. • This case led to the "Lau Remedies" that defined the appropriate approaches, methods, and procedures when: 1. Identifying and evaluating minority students' English language skills. 2. Providing appropriate instructional treatments. 3. Deciding when ELs are ready to attend mainstream classes.	• Families should fully understand the educational rights of their children. They should become familiar with the types of programs offered at the district and school levels. • Teacher–family meetings should create opportunities for families to understand their rights and roles within the context of the school. • Parent leaders should become members of the evaluation committee. • Language bridging personnel should be available to provide language support for families.

Table 1.1. History of Family Engagement in the United States (*continued*)

Cases	Implications for CLD Families	Implications for Families and Schools
	4. Determining what professional standards must be met by teachers of ELs.	
Castañeda v. Pickard (1981)	• While this case undermined the role of bilingual education, it established a test to evaluate the actions schools take to support the language and academic needs of EL populations. • Programs must be based on educational theory. • Effective implementation must ensure necessary resources and personnel. • Programs should undergo evaluation procedures to determine their effectiveness in meeting the needs of ELs.	• As families gain a deeper understanding of the English language programs currently established to serve the academic and language needs of their children, they should engage in conversations with the school to understand how the program is structured and implemented. • Families should be aware of the professional credentials of the personnel serving their children. • Results and action plans from program evaluations should be communicated to families.

Educational Legislation

Educational researchers contributed to legislation promoting parent involvement in schools.

Project Headstart (1964)	• This legislation was enacted to assist in the education of "disadvantaged children in the inner cities" (Hiatt, 1994, p. 35).
Elementary and Secondary Act (1965)	• This act required that parents be allowed to become part of advisory boards and actively participate in classroom activities.
Education for All Handicapped Children Act (1975)	• This act, designed by teachers, parents, children, and specialists, required parents to be active participants in determining their children's individual education plans.
Goals 2000	• Enacted by Bill Clinton in 1994, the purpose of this bill was to provide resources to states and communities to ensure that all students succeed academically. • Parent involvement was included as one of the goals.

NCLB (2001)	• This act reauthorized the Elementary and Secondary Act. • It provided parents with more rights and responsibilities. • The law called for more parent notification, strategies to assist in parent involvement, as well as holding parents accountable for their children's education. • Local Family Information Centers (LFICs) should have been formed, but this part of the act was never fully funded by the legislation. Therefore, the intention of educating parents on how to "play a more active role" in their children's education was not properly enacted.
American Recovery and Reinvestment Act (2009)	• This act allocated funding for home visits, which provided parenting coaches to young, at-risk families.
Every Student Succeeds Act (2015)	• This act shifted the vocabulary of "parent engagement" to "family engagement," as family compositions have changed since the Elementary and Secondary Act of 1965. • ESSA Title I goals included "to establish the agency's expectations and objectives for meaningful parent and family involvement" (Henderson, n.d., p. 2). • Districts are required to use these funds for professional development, home-based programs, information dissemination, collaboration with community-based organizations, or other activities that promote family engagement.

Sources: Henderson, n.d.; Hiatt, 1994; Hiatt-Michael, 2010; Klein, Mitchell, Samuels, & Blad, 2017; Lyons, 1995; National Council of La Raza, 2007; Woyshner, 2009; Wright, n.d.

The language found within the decisions of these cases provide educators with the "power" to advocate for CLD students. However, how often do we learn about these cases in the foundation courses of our teacher preparation, and (assuming we do) then fail to reflect on, act on, or enter into conversations with our colleagues about what they mean in current practice? Often what we as educators are legally bound to is far removed from our work in the classroom. Yet, the cases and decisions are there to protect our students and families at the most basic level.

Driven by Reform: Stalled by Complexity

The roots of reform for parental involvement and engagement driven by federal, state, and local policies date back to the 1930s when the White House convened the Conference on Child Health and Protection. According to Berger (1991), the conference envisioned the role of parent involvement as "educating" parents on the norms necessary for their children to be successful in school. This included how children should be raised and how they should behave if they were to be counted as important in society. At this point in time, parental involvement was seen as an add-on, with the goal that "immigrant and indigent families assimilate into middle-class society, adopting the values and attitudes of the prevailing culture" (Price-Mitchell, 2009, p. 11).

The Civil Rights Act of 1964 added to the conversation on parental involvement by further describing what parental engagement should look like. The recommendations, according to Price-Mitchell (2009), were grounded in "helping ethnic minorities adopt the values of the dominant race" (p. 11). The Title I program shifted the conversation toward jumpstarting services to low-income parents and, for the first time, recognized that culture and class dynamics should be considered as assets within parental involvement programs, given that ethnic minority parents would also need to be involved in making governance and policy decisions (Price-Mitchell, 2009). Most U.S. educators are familiar with the *No Child Left Behind (NCLB) Act*, which sought to mandate that all schools work on increasing parental involvement in order to increase academic success for all learners (NCLB, 2002). Yet NCLB failed to provide any clear and practical guidance on how such efforts could be carried out.

The reform agendas summarized in Table 1.1 are still attempting to inform schools about the importance parents play within their contexts. To date, however, these agendas have failed to move the needle sufficiently toward achieving the equitable engagement of families. Each has failed to understand and adequately account for the complexity of school settings. Every school setting has a unique population and sociopolitical context that is ever changing. In addition, each state, district, school, and classroom has its own values and interpretation of policy and reform, and defines policy and regulation through the lens of its own assumptions, priorities, and needs. It is within this complex context that conversations in the field surrounding models began to take shape. Models of parental engagement and involvement emerged in response to legislation and recommendations.

Context Matters: Parental Engagement Models, Politics, and Lived Realities

Current models, frameworks, and philosophies of parental engagement and involvement are heavily centered on educating parents on what research finds they need to do in order to positively influence their child's development and academic achievement. Each provides educators with points of departure that may have an impact on the involvement and engagement of parents within their own setting. Such models are heavily focused on what makes an "engaged and involved parent." When parents do not fit the model, guidance is provided on how they can be educated to become better parents. Although each model provides indicators or principles for attending to the spirit of collaboration, trust, and relationship building, there is a void as to how enactment of the model would position the conversation around identifying the assets, strengths, and knowledge that parents bring to the school and classroom setting.

Table 1.2 provides a brief look at some the most prevalent models, frameworks, and philosophies currently found in the research and practical literature. We have reflected on and summarized the contributions each makes to the field on parental engagement. Each leaves room for moving beyond current thinking and moving toward detailing processes for operationalization and enactment within diverse school settings. For this reason, we also pose questions for reflection and make recommendations for going one step beyond.

DO UNTO THEM: UNIDIRECTIONAL MODELS FOR PARENTAL ENGAGEMENT AND INVOLVEMENT

We began this chapter by taking a moment to reflect on how the unique situations of individual families might influence our conceptualization and characterization of parental involvement/engagement. The field of parental involvement and engagement continues to fumble through research studies and on-the-ground programs, attempting to make sense of the terms and operationalize the role of parents within the school and classroom context. Given that active engagement of parents and caregivers in the academic world of the child is seen as an effective strategy for increasing academic success, school districts rush to ensure a proper plan is in place, especially during this time of accountability. However, finding a definition that is agreed upon has been difficult for researchers and educators alike.

A plethora of definitions permeate the field. Different states and local contexts have their own models, frameworks, and designated policies and strategies. The various terms and definitions are sociopolitical in nature, having evolved from a particular sociocultural and

Table 1.2. Models, Frameworks, and Philosophies

Joyce Epstein's Six Types of Parent Involvement (Epstein, 2001; Epstein et al., 2002)		
Basic Principles	**Contributions**	**Questions to Be Posed**
1. Parenting: Help all families establish home environments to support children as students. 2. Communicating: Design effective forms of school-to-home and home-to-school communications about school programs and children's progress. 3. Volunteering: Recruit and organize parent help and support. 4. Learning at home: Provide information and ideas to families about how to help students at home with homework and other curriculum-related activities, decisions, and planning. 5. Decisionmaking: Include families as participants in school decisions and develop parent leaders and representatives.	• Provides a framework for guiding schools toward involving parents in their children's education. • Recognizes the role of parents in student success. • Provides school-centric approach to parent involvement. • Promotes bidirectional communication through PTA and advising councils.	• How does the model account for dynamics of power within the educational context? • In what ways does the model guide school personnel on alternative ways of involvement? • What strategies does this model promote to discover experiences and knowledge that is culturally bound? • How do teachers foster the family's culture while encouraging school–family connections? • Although bidirectional communication is encouraged, how do families help teachers make decisions about their children's education?
A Cord of Three Strands: A New Approach to Parent Engagement in Schools (Hong & Anyon, 2011)		
1. Induction: Introduce parents to the complex world of schools. 2. Integration: Develop parent presence in school communities. 3. Investment: Support emerging leaders on the continuous journey of parent engagement.	• Moves from individual orientation to collective orientation. • Heavily bound by networks and relationships.	• What practical ideas does this model give teachers to help engage families? • In what ways are conditions set within classroom structures to make engagement occur?

Basic Principles	Contributions	Questions to Be Posed
	• Grounded in parents' knowledge and expertise. • Moves toward school personnel recognizing assets and resources of parents.	• How will the cultural and language backgrounds of CLD parents be explored?

Powerful Partnerships:

A Teacher's Guide to Engage Families in Student Success

(Mapp, Carver, & Lander, 2017)

Basic Principles	Contributions	Questions to Be Posed
1. Condition 1: Directly linked to learning. 2. Condition 2: Builds relationships between teachers and parents, and between parents. 3. Condition 3: Collaborative, with equal participation and input from teachers, families, and students. 4. Condition 4: Honors families' home languages, cultures, and experiences. 5. Condition 5: Interactive, providing many and varied opportunities to learn together.	• Takes into consideration that teachers come to school with core beliefs that they must examine before working with families. • Sheds light on commonly held teacher beliefs and attitudes toward CLD families. • Focuses on collaboration with communities and families.	• In what ways does this model suggest teachers connect with CLD families? • How do teachers honor families' core beliefs to engage them in their children's education? • In what ways can family engagement be more authentic in teaching and learning contexts?

political context. They have become imbued with undertones of frequently unspoken messages about what's possible, practical, and desirable. According to Price-Mitchell's (2009) review of current research, parental involvement has been variously defined in the following ways (p. 12):

- The degree of communication parents have with teachers and the school about their children (Epstein, 1991; Miedel & Reynolds, 1999)
- Parent–child interaction around homework (Clark, 1993; Cooper, Lindsay, & Nye, 2000)

- Aspirations parents hold and communicate for their children's academic achievement (Bloom, 1980; Lopez, 2001a; Lopez, 2001b)
- Parents' participation in school activities (Mapp, 1999; Stevenson & Baker, 1987)
- Parental rules imposed in the home that affect education (Keith, Reimers, Fehrmann, Pottebaum, & Aubey, 1986)
- Developing a supportive home environment (Desforges & Abouchaar, 2003; Xu, 2001)

To these, the following definitions can be added:

- Volunteering at the school, communicating with teachers, assisting with homework, and attending school events, such as performances or parent–teacher conferences (Epstein et al., 2009)
- Supporting the learner academically at home (Lopez, Scribner, & Mahitivanichcha, 2001)

Currently, the most adopted model for guiding parental involvement decisions in schools is Epstein's (1987, 1990, 1995) six categories for working with parents. Epstein's model (see Table 1.2) has been adopted by the National Parent Teacher Association. The model guides educators toward exploring explicit ways for parents to support their children toward academic success. Epstein's model asks parents to think about ways for establishing a home environment that supports their children as learners, and it includes recommendations on family literacy, health and nutrition, and training on other pertinent ways that the home can become a learning place for the child. Recommendations for communication are also provided, such as having translators for conferences, scheduling regular conferences, and providing newsletters that keep parents informed. Parents volunteering and becoming active with PTA/PTO, advisory councils, or district-level committees are highly valued. Epstein's model sets the stage for a high-quality, school-centric approach to involving and engaging families. However, an exploration of where the model has made assumptions about CLD parents/caregivers is needed.

Over time, the term *parental involvement* has come to be viewed as a one-dimensional lens of what counts as involvement and participation. The more recent term *parental engagement* has emerged to take its place in current research. According to Marilyn Price-Mitchell (2009), this new term's focus is on creating school contexts where parents play a role in the education of their child not merely by responding to invitations to participate, but by serving as equal stakeholders and sharing power in the decisionmaking process. Yet Price-Mitchell states, "[T]he shift in language has yet to change the fragmented focus of research, and many schools continue to emphasize participation and volunteerism over partnership and engagement" (2009, p. 13). The complexity faced by all parties in clearly defining a model for engaging parents/caregivers leaves room for redefining the sphere of what it means to engage or partner with families within school contexts. Lacking in current research and literature is clear evidence on how to get past unidirectional models that position the school and educators as experts.

Existing models that seek to engage families have helped lay a foundation for strengthening school–family–community relationships. Each model has provided ideas that have improved school–community dynamics over the years; however, these models tend to be school-driven and prescriptive. Rather than create a new model or revise an existing model, we suggest hitting the pause button. Often when a problem occurs, it can be more enticing to fix it by proposing a solution rather than by searching for the root of the problem—especially if the person seeking solutions is part of the problem. In other words, before teachers and administrators devise a detailed community engagement plan that includes quantifiable goals directly linked to student learning outcomes, they might consider beginning by recognizing institutional biases that the school upholds in its communication with families.

We must seek first to see and understand the community, caregivers, families, and parents that are being served within the school. We must be committed to dialoging as a staff before designing a year-long calendar of events. We must be honest with ourselves in order to recognize systematic barriers. How is current policy marginalizing families? As educators, how can we develop a greater sociological imagination (Mills, 1959) and recognize ways our own lived experiences are shaping our opinions and actions? These are tough questions that don't link to a detailed model, but they begin to establish a community based on vulnerability and transparency that has the potential to reveal itself in each interaction. Chapter 6 provides a resource for reflecting on how to take what we know about parental involvement and engagement and apply it to practice. The framework will guide you, as the educator, to re-envision and chart new pathways for conversations about what is possible with parents. When re-envisioning involvement and engagement, we must foster a paradigm shift that looks at involvement and engagement not as roles among stakeholders in schooling, but as *relationships* that build on each other to create an ecology within the school that values all knowledge and voices. How might such a shift focus our attention on interactions between human beings rooted in trust, love, and support?

BEYOND THE MODELS: FAMILIES AS EQUAL CONTRIBUTORS FOR SOCIAL AND ACADEMIC GROWTH

For decades we have continued to conduct extensive research on parental involvement and engagement, coining new terms, crafting new language, and putting together new handbooks on how to build better partnerships/relationships between parents and schools. What has been absent in this research is how to move beyond the school-centric conversations of what we should do. As authors, our vision is to provide a new paradigm that shifts the discourse toward envisioning a more organic approach to making decisions about engaging in reciprocal exchanges through ongoing conversation.

A move toward a more inclusive paradigm will require that we explore literature and research that has often been left outside of the boundaries we have arbitrarily set on the topic of parental involvement and engagement. Toward that end, we are framing our discussions and the foundation of this book on theory that brings forth deeper thinking about social and cultural capital, relational trust, cultural competency as a skill, cultural compatibility as a cultivation of learning about each other, and *hope*. We borrow from theory that pushes past limiting mindsets and rhetoric that have created a system driven by deficit thinking about the communities and families of the most marginalized populations we serve. Expanding our conceptualization of family engagement has the potential to enhance our understanding about how to create equitable spaces where parents and educators define parental engagement together, using the culture and language of all parties. In the next section, we discuss the work of theorists and researchers who contributed to our knowledge base for reimagining what is possible in school–parent/caregiver relationships.

Making Walls Visible: Reframing for Equity

Current voices on moving beyond models and frameworks that exclusively value dominant ways of thinking and knowing ask us as educators to question oppressive ideologies and explore how they may intersect and impact the lives of CLD learners and their caregivers/families. In order to move forward in engaging parents and valuing their voices in school contexts, attention must be focused on maximizing their potent and undervalued contributions (Herrera, 2016). Solorzano (1998) posits that to leave behind oppressive ways of thinking and acting within school contexts, educators would benefit from respecting the merit and value of what the learner and family bring to the space.

Alcoff (2006, 2015) argues that we tend to designate identity based on what we see; this tendency is inescapable and, left unchecked, has the potential of bounding the way we interact with caregivers and families. The attributions that we as educators make are a product of our socialization throughout life. Our attitudes and beliefs about those who care for students, as well as our valuing of them, become part of our schema that guides how we view and act in the world. As educators, we thrive on stability and patterns for acting. Moving beyond current thinking will require us to ask difficult questions about where parents have been positioned in our individual and shared schemas.

Solorzano (1998) has written that despite our rhetoric in education and the pivotal court decisions on the topic, our schools continue to reproduce inequalities in our society. For Yosso (2005), achieving an equitable education for all must encompass new perspectives on schooling, students, and caregivers. This will necessitate enhanced awareness about the ways economic, social, cultural, and political power shape our human relationships and how we interact with the world around us. In part, enhanced awareness and new perspectives will need to encompass engaging caregivers and families from more equitable positions of power. The structural arrangements currently in place will need to be scrutinized and reframed to become more democratic in nature. A new, shared vision of what is possible, guided by mutual respect and trust, has the potential of opening new pathways for mutually beneficial relationships.

Thinking Ourselves Away in the Pursuit of Relational Trust

When attempting to understand social issues, sociologist C. Wright Mills (1959) argues the importance of recognizing the history and multiple contexts of a given situation while attempting to "think our-selves away" from our own ways of seeing and doing. Taking this tact will provide a greater understanding of the complicated nature of the situation and the importance of recognizing multiple perspectives. He refers to this process as developing one's *sociological imagination*. How, as educators, can we begin to "think ourselves away" from our own routines and entrenched ways of seeing, in order to develop the abil-ity to recognize circumstances that may be affecting the situation? Whether we like to admit it or not, our responses to families are often based on our own comfort levels, ways of seeing the world, and judg-ments about how things ought to be.

One of the outcomes of broadening our sociological imagina-tion and fostering an ethic of care in our schools is the emergence of relational trust. Bryk and Schneider (2002) discuss the importance of establishing rapport based on relationships within the context of schooling. They discuss the mistrust that often exists between educa-tors and families based on (1) educator perceptions of family choices as not supporting learning and (2) families feeling misunderstood or judged by school personnel.

> This lack of trust between teachers and parents—often exacerbated by race and class differences—makes it difficult for these groups to maintain a genuine dialogue about shared concerns. The resultant miscommuni-cations tend to reinforce existing prejudices and undermine constructive efforts by teachers and parents to build relational ties around the interest of children. Instead of working together . . . teachers and parents find themselves operating in isolation or, in the worst cases, in opposition to one another. (Bryk & Schneider, 2002, p. 6)

Bryk and Schneider emphasize relational trust as the core component of enhancing ties between educators and families.

Differing from positional trust, which is based on status or rank-ing, relational trust is built through daily interactions and exchanges that are authentic and reliant upon: listening and valuing one an-other, a willingness to go beyond our formally designated roles, and demonstrated consistency between what is said and done (Bryk & Schneider, 2002). Relational trust is more lasting and authentic than positional trust because it requires a vested commitment to another person. Relationships between families and educators are a collective promise built on trust that cannot be found when we focus exclusively on learning gains and participation at school events. Rather than the result of years of training, experience, or willingness to serve in our professional capacities, trust is something earned based on how we treat one another. When families feel seen, heard, and appreciated, relational trust begins to weave together schools, families, and communities in equitable and sustained ways.

Context, Conditions, and Positionality

Relational trust is impossible to achieve, however, without the cultural understanding and recognition of our own positionality, particularly with regard to privilege or capital. Social theorist Pierre Bourdieu (1986) argues that capital impacts one's social status and position in society. Going beyond the familiar, economic notion of capital, Bourdieu examines *cultural capital* (nonfinancial assets), as comprised of symbolic elements such as educational degrees, fashion, language, and mannerisms that reinforce a sense of collective identity among individuals who share similar backgrounds.

Cultural capital, according to Bourdieu (1986), exists in three states: embodied, objectified, and institutionalized. A person's accent would be an example of embodied cultural capital. That is, some audiences tend to believe that a British English accent is valuable and such an accent is, therefore, a form of embodied capital. Objectified capital is often more tangible. For example, a person's collection of books, to many, is an instance of objectified cultural capital. Institutionalized capital is frequently conferred by the dominant culture. One such example would be a degree earned from a prestigious university.

For Bourdieu (1986), each form of cultural capital reinforces homogenous social grouping and social inequality. He further theorizes that cultural capital fosters deeply rooted habits and ways of interacting in and relating to the world that he calls *habitus*. Likening habitus to the playing of a sport, Bourdieu has explained that athletes simply know how to maneuver the field due to their habitus, which was derived from cultural capital.

Beyond the notion of sports and playing an athletic game, Bourdieu (1986) examines the "game" of life as a means to understanding social hierarchies. Using the term *fields*, Bourdieu analyzes how society is broken into settings, such as politics, religion, or education. Each setting (field) has its own set of guiding principles. Individuals utilize their cultural capital and habitus to navigate these spaces. Bourdieu (1977) has employed these and other theoretical constructs when examining social inequalities that are reproduced within the context of schooling. The application of Bourdieu's ideas helps explain the marginalization that CLD families face when trying to navigate school settings without having the cultural capital and habitus valued by dominant school culture to freely and confidently maneuver existing procedures and nuances.

Rios-Aguilar, Kiyama, Gravitt, and Moll (2011) have argued that there are two distinct forms of capital: social and cultural. Capital, in this sense, involves not only what one invests in a goal (e.g., financial assets, time) but also the rewards that ensue from the attainment of that goal. From an educational perspective, we can think of social capital as ways in which a caregiver creates and sustains relationships with, for example, teachers, counselors, and administrators, to enhance educational outcomes for her or his child. Cultural capital, on the other hand, is a valuing of unique ways of knowing and being in the world that are cultivated over time within a given culture.

Caregivers and families are likely to benefit from strategies that enhance their social capital in relation to schools and school systems (Rios-Aguilar et al., 2011). On one hand, caregivers who learn strategies that enhance their social capital benefit because they expand their social base by building relationships with those who better understand the context of schools; they also gain insights into how to navigate this social base. On the other hand, children/students benefit because their teachers and counselors may plan and implement interventions in ways that result in, for example, better achievement scores. Utilizing social capital opens up pathways for understanding and valuing what caregivers and parents bring to the teaching and learning context.

Similarly, caregivers possess and can enhance the extent of their cultural capital (Rios-Aguilar et al., 2011). Consider what aspects of a culture prompt members to build cultural capital that is valued by the society's institutions. Some cultures, for instance, value respect for authority figures and both independent and collaborative ways of learning and knowing. Each of these cultural values (assimilated as cultural capital) are typically valued by the institutions of Western schooling and education. Accordingly, members of such cultures who are familiar with these values interact with peers and educators in ways that are judged positively, as bringing high levels of cultural capital to the classroom and/or the education of their children.

Caregivers and families bring both types of capital to the education setting. Both can be used to bolster family engagement. Social and cultural capital can be accessed through caregivers' *funds of knowledge*, defined in the literature by Luis Moll and colleagues (Moll, Amanti, Neff,

& González, 1992) as the experiential knowledge we can document based on the activities carried out in the daily lives of families. These historical accounts of the experiences of families (e.g., household practices, employment, children rearing practices) can provide educators with a foundation of *capital* to draw on as they let go of deficit perspectives about CLD students and caregivers/families.

For example, very seldom do educators bring the migrant student experience into learning. Children who grow up counting rows in fields to calculate when the day's work will be finished and it will be time to go home (whether that means a 10-hour or 12-hour day), skinning snakes to compare lengths and rattles to determine their age, and filling bushel baskets with strawberries or apples gain science and math knowledge through lived experiences. Yet seldom are these experiences brought into classrooms as critical funds for valuing what is known. It is for this reason Moll and colleagues argue that conversations and research emphasizing *funds of knowledge* need to reconsider notions of social and cultural capital, through which educators may be able to better understand these funds.

Yosso (2005) further posits that attending to the inequities that exist within cultural contexts moves the conversation toward understanding *capital* from a lens situated in familial and community wealth. Efforts such as these shift Bourdieu's ideas on cultural *capital* to be more cognizant of, and responsive to, CLD populations.

Get to Know Me: Engagement as Hope

> [I]f I do not love the world—if I do not love life—if I do not love
> people—I cannot enter into dialogue. (Freire, 2003, p. 90)

According to Freire (2003), love will lead to dialogue. Dialogue becomes a dynamic and equitable exchange of ideas that fosters our love the world and its people. When love and dialogue converge, transformation ensues at its most fundamental level, thus leading us toward the process of individual humanization.

We are challenged to disrupt fixed educational transactions centered around top-down approaches. Such approaches maintain the status quo by relegating CLD families' voices to the periphery, preventing them from partaking in the dynamic process of dialogue. The inclusivity of loving the world and its people (Freire, 2003) inspires us to act and disrupt hegemonic learning and teaching practices as schools attempt to reach out to families whose experiences, languages, and identities are not congruent with the "norm." Authentic love, guided by principles of social justice, inclusivity, and equity, cannot occur without hope and the genuine desire to listen and learn from the families we serve. When we strive to understand and see through one another's eyes, we are better able to incorporate a multitude of experiences and narratives in the curricula we write and the schools we build.

CONCLUSION

As educators, engaging with parents and families may seem like an overwhelming goal. Stepping outside the classroom walls, when time is always limited, can feel like an impossible task. Yet imagine what can be gained if we allow ourselves the opportunity to explore the cultural and linguistic assets and life experiences of our students' caregivers and families! Gaining personal and interpersonal awareness, sensitivity, and skills positions us to truly *hear* what CLD families tell us. Opening up pathways with caregivers/families allows us to develop greater levels of understanding, build relationships, and discover strengths. It also paves the way for us to more thoroughly explore and maximize the assets learners bring to the classroom.

With cultural documentation and understanding that results from dialogue, we can plan and deliver instruction in ways that reflect our learning gained from caregivers/families. It is through this process that we are best able to enact effective, culturally responsive teaching. Vygotsky (1978) asserts that all learners benefit from instruction that takes them one step beyond their current level of understanding. Opportunities for maximizing student potential come from our knowing and using the culture and language of the student's home to move learning forward in meaningful, relevant ways.

Beyond those skills, Tharp and Dalton (2007) remind us that our goal as educators is to keep moving forward and building our skills and dispositions toward *cultural compatibility*—a sense of belonging comes from our mutual perspective on what we value in the world. Often two people do not always value the same things. However, when educators reflect, explore, and reshape their understanding through the lens of the families/caregivers sitting across from them, they open up possibilities for both parties to understand each other.

Cultural compatibility begins with our ability as educators to accept what we don't understand and value what is there.

REFERENCES

Alcoff, L. (2006). *Visible identities: Race, gender and the self.* New York, NY: Oxford University.

Alcoff, L. (2015). *The future of Whiteness.* Cambridge and Malden, MA: Polity.

Berger, E. H. (1991). Parent involvement: Yesterday and today. *The Elementary School Journal, 91*(3), 209–219.

Bloom, B. S. (1980). The new direction for educational research: Alterable variables. *Phi Delta Kappan, 61*(6), 382–385.

Bourdieu, P. (1977). *Reproduction in education, society and culture.* Beverly Hills, CA: Sage.

Bourdieu, P. (1986). The forms of capital. In J. Richardson (Ed.), *Handbook of theory and research for the sociology of education* (pp. 241–258). New York, NY: Greenwood.

Brown v. Board of Education, 347 U.S. 463 (1954).

Bryk, A. S., & Schneider, B. (2002). *Trust in schools: A core resource for improvement.* New York, NY: Russell Sage Foundation.

Bus, A., van Ijzendoorn, M., & Pellegrini, A. (1995). Joint book reading makes for success in learning to read: A meta-analysis on intergenerational transmission of literacy. *Review of Educational Research, 65*(1), 1–21.

Castañeda v. Pickard, 781 F.2d 456 (1978).

Clark, R. (1993). Homework-focused parenting practices that positively affect student achievement. In N. F. Chavkin (Ed.), *Families and schools in a pluralistic society* (pp. 85–105). Albany, NY: State University of New York Press.

Cooper, H., Lindsay, J. J., & Nye, B. (2000). Homework in the home: How student, family, and parenting-style differences relate to the homework process. *Contemporary Educational Psychology, 25*(4), 464–487.

Desforges, C., & Abouchaar, A. (2003). *The impact of parental involvement, parental support and family education on pupil achievement and adjustment: A literature review.* Nottingham, UK: Department for Education and Skills.

Epstein, J. L. (1987). Toward a theory of family-school connections: Teacher practices and parent involvement. In K. Hurrelmann, F. Kaufmann, & F. Losel (Eds.), *Social intervention: Potential and constraints* (pp. 121–136). New York, NY: DeGruyter.

Epstein, J. L. (1990). School and family connections: Theory, research, and implications for integrating sociologies of education and family. In D. G. Unger & M. B. Sussman (Eds.), *Families in community settings: Interdisciplinary perspectives* (pp. 99–126). New York, NY: Haworth Press.

Epstein, J. L. (1991). Effects on student achievement of teachers' practices of parent involvement. In S. Silvern (Ed.), *Advances in reading/language research: Literacy through family, community, and school interaction* (Vol. 5, pp. 261–276). Greenwich, CT: JAI Press.

Epstein, J. L. (1995). School/family/community partnerships. *Phi Delta Kappan,76*(9), 701–712.

Epstein, J. L. (2001). *School, family, and community partnerships: Preparing educators and improving schools.* Boulder, CO: Westview.

Epstein, J. L., Sanders, M. G., Simon, B. S., Salinas, K. C., Jansorn, N. R., & Van Voorhis, F. L. (2002). *School, family, and community partnerships: Your handbook for action* (2nd ed.). Thousand Oaks, CA: Corwin Press.

Epstein, J. L., Sanders, M. G., Simon, B. S., Salinas, K. C., Jansorn, N. R., & Van Voorhis, F. L. (2009). *School, family, and community partnerships: Your handbook for action.* Thousand Oaks, CA: Corwin Press.

Freire, P. (2003). *Pedagogy of the oppressed* (30th anniversary ed.). New York: Continuum.

Henderson, A. T. (n.d.). *Quick brief on family engagement in every student succeeds act (ESSA) of 2015.* Retrieved from ra.nea.org/wp-content/uploads/2016 /06/FCE-in-ESSA-in-Brief.pdf

Herrera, S. (2016). *Biography-driven culturally responsive teaching* (2nd ed.). New York, NY: Teachers College Press.

Hiatt, D. B. (1994). Parent involvement in American public schools: An historical perspective 1642–1994. *The School Community Journal, 4*(2), 27–38.

Hiatt-Michael, D. (2001). Parent involvement in American public schools: A historic perspective 1642–2000. In S. Redding & L. G. Thomas (Eds.), *The community of the school* (pp. 247–258). Lincoln, IL: Academic Development Institute.

Hill, N. E., & Taylor, L. C. (2004). Parental school involvement and children's academic achievement: Pragmatics and issues. *Current Directions in Psychological Science, 13*(4), 161–164.

Hong, S., & Anyon, J. (2011). *A cord of three strands: A new approach to parent engagement in schools.* Cambridge, MA: Harvard Education Press.

Jeynes, W. H. (2003). A meta-analysis: The effects of parental involvement on minority children's academic achievement. *Education & Urban Society, 35*(2), 202–218.

Keith, T. Z., Reimers, T. M., Fehrmann, P. G., Pottebaum, S. M., & Aubey, L. W. (1986). Parental involvement, homework, and TV times: Direct and indirect effects on high school achievement. *Journal of Educational Psychology, 78*(5), 373–380.

Klein, A., Mitchell, C., Samuels, C. A., & Blad, E. (2017, January 10). *The Obama administration's imprint on K-12 policy: A roundup.* Retrieved from www.edweek.org/ew/section/multimedia/the-obama-administrations -imprint-on-k-12-policy.html

LaRocque, M., Kleiman, I., & Darling, S. M. (2011). Parental involvement: The missing link in school achievement. *Preventing School Failure, 53*(3), 115–122. doi:10.1080/10459880903472876

Lau v. Nichols, 414 U.S. 563 (1974).

Lopez, G. R. (2001a, April). *On whose terms? Understanding involvement through the eyes of migrant parents.* Paper presented at the annual meeting of the American Educational Research Association, Seattle, WA.

Lopez, G. R. (2001b). The value of hard work: Lessons on parent involvement from an (im)migrant household. *Harvard Educational Review, 71*(3), 416–438.

Lopez, G. R., Scribner, J. D., & Mahitivanichcha, K. (2001). Redefining parental involvement: Lessons from high performing migrant-impacted schools. *American Educational Research Journal, 38*(2), 253–228.

Lyons, J. (1995). The past and future directions of federal bilingual education policy. In O. García & C. Baker (Eds.), *Policy and practice in bilingual education: Extending the foundations* (pp. 1–15). Clevedon, UK: Multilingual Matters.

Mapp, K. L. (1999). *Making the connection between families and schools: Why and how parents are involved in their children's education* (Unpublished doctoral dissertation). Harvard University, Cambridge, MA.

Mapp, K. L., Carver, I., & Lander, J. (2017). *Powerful partnerships: A teacher's guide to engaging families for student success.* New York, NY: Scholastic.

Meyer v. Nebraska, 262 U.S. 390 (1923).

Miedel, W. T., & Reynolds, A. J. (1999). Parent involvement in early intervention for disadvantaged children. Does it matter? *Journal of School Psychology, 37*(4), 379–402.

Mills, C. W. (1959). *The sociological imagination.* New York, NY: Oxford University Press.

Moll, L. C., Amanti, C., Neff, D., & González, N. (1992). Funds of knowledge for teaching: Using a qualitative approach to connect homes and classrooms. *Theory into Practice, 31*(2), 132–141.

National Council of La Raza (NCLR). (2007). *Parental involvement in the No Child Left Behind Act* (Fact Sheet). Retrieved from publications.unidosus .org/bitstream/handle/123456789/858/FS_ParentalInvol.pdf?sequence =1&isAllowed=y

No Child Left Behind Act of 2001, P.L. 107–110, 20 U.S.C. § 6319 (2002).

Prentice, A. R., & Houston, S. E. (1975). *Family, school, and society.* Toronto, Ontario, Canada: Oxford University Press.

Price-Mitchell, M. (2009). Boundary dynamics: Implications for building parent-school partnerships. *School Community Journal, 19*(2), 9–26.

Rios-Aguilar, C., Kiyama, J. M., Gravitt, M., & Moll, L. C. (2011). Funds of knowledge for the poor and forms of capital for the rich? A capital approach to examining funds of knowledge. *School Field, 9*(2), 163–184. doi:10.1177/1477878511409776

Schlossman, S. (1976). Before home start: Notes toward a history of parent education in America, 1897–1929. *Harvard Educational Review, 46*(3), 436–467.

Solorzano, D. G. (1998). Critical race theory, race and gender microaggressions, and the experience of Chicana and Chicano scholars. *International Journal of Qualitative Studies in Education, 11*(1), 121–136.

Stevenson, D. L., & Baker, D. P. (1987). The family-school relation and the child's school performance. *Child Development, 58*(5), 1348–1357.

Tharp, R. G., & Dalton, S. S. (2007). Orthodoxy, cultural compatibility, and universals in education. *Comparative Education, 43*(1), 53–70.

Vygotsky, L. S. (1978). *Mind in society: The development of higher psychological processes* (M. Cole, V. John-Steiner, S. Scribner, & E. Souberman, Eds.). Cambridge, MA: Harvard University Press.

Watson, T. N., & Bogotch, I. (2015). Reframing parent involvement: What should urban school leaders do differently? *Leadership and Policy in Schools, 14*(3), 257–278.

Wilder, S. (2014). Effects of parental involvement on academic achievement: A meta-synthesis. *Educational Review, 66*(3), 377–397.

Woyshner, C. A. (2009). *The national PTA, race, and civic engagement, 1897–1970.* Columbus: Ohio State University Press.

Wright, W. E. (n.d.). *Landmark court rulings regarding English language learners.* Retrieved from www.colorincolorado.org/article/landmark-court-rulings-regarding-english-language-learners

Xu, J. (2001, April). *Middle school family involvement in urban settings: Perspectives from minority students and their families.* Paper presented at the annual meeting of the American Educational Research Association, Seattle, WA.

CHAPTER 2

"They Just Don't Show Up"

What we say and what we do ultimately comes back to us, so let us own our responsibility, place it in our own hands and carry it with dignity and strength.

—Gloria Anzaldúa (1981), p. 171

Key Concepts: languaging, labeling theory, white privilege, transgenerational narratives, binary ways of seeing

---

INTRODUCTION

Language is a powerful tool. When exploring the construct of language, we must attend to the social and physical environment (Vygotsky, 1962). Our linguistic actions are confined within the context of how we make sense of the world around us. Individuals exhibit an inherent need to create as well as adopt specific linguistic features in order to subscribe or identify themselves as members of a particular group. Language, as a social construct, features both communication and socialization as primary functions. According to Carroll (1956), language shapes what we think and determines what we think about. Needless to say, the way we use language can transform our knowledge and decisionmaking processes. At its best, it helps us create liberating spaces of creativity and thought; at its worst, it endorses oppressive linguistic practices. These ideas play a crucial role in every aspect of our lives, particularly within the context of education. If language is conceptualized as a free entity with "no fixed boundaries, but rather is made of hybrids and endless varieties resulting from language being creative, expressive, contact and dialogue-based, debated, negotiated, and mediated" (Shohamy, 2006, p. 5), then we must consider the instructional implications of how language is used in schools (e.g., collaboration, focus on meaning).

Language is a multifaceted construct that is inherently linked to students and their families' identities and narratives. Schools should celebrate the diversity of their students' languages as part of their cultural identities. If educators view language as a significant tool of instruction, then instructional language practices should be carefully analyzed in order to disrupt hegemonic teaching approaches. As teachers, we begin with the conscious decision to invite and value the cognitive, linguistic, academic, and sociocultural contributions of every family represented in our classroom (Herrera, 2016). We then find ways of disrupting our preconceived notions of how language is utilized in order to create spaces where students and families are able to establish and negotiate their own sense of languaging (Shohamy, 2006). According to Shohamy (2006), *languaging* encompasses every single tool we, as humans, use to make sense and communicate with the world (e.g., gestures, looks, clothing, music). Educators must explore the multiple ways in which language currently is utilized in the classroom, and reflect on how it could be used to build stronger connections between schools and families. Consider the following scenario:

Mi Abuelita & Hawthorne's *Scarlet Letter*

It was my first week of school in the United States, and my English III teacher gave me a copy of Hawthorne's *Scarlet Letter*. A friend was able to translate the teacher's instructions for me and explained that we would have quizzes every week, a midterm, and a final assignment based on the novel. I had only been in the country for a few months, and now I was expected to fully understand this text and meet the required learning standards. I came home that afternoon anxious, and I told *Mamá Erito, mi abuelita* (my grandmother), what I was expected to do. She always offered peaceful words in moments of uncertainty; she had always been *mi faro guia* (my guiding light).

Después de la cena (After dinner), I sat down at my tiny desk. I opened the novel, grabbed my Spanish-English dictionary, and began the daunting task of looking up every word on the first page. However, some words were impossible to find. When I finished, my eyes flew back to the beginning of the page, and I began to read, sadly realizing that I was even more confused than when I first had started. I quickly learned that a movie had been made, and my parents drove me to a local video store to locate the movie version of the book. After watching the movie, I felt frustrated. Looking at the questions in my assignment, I didn't know how to answer them. I didn't have the language to offer a cohesive analysis of the characters, setting, or plot, or to provide a coherent critique of the author's purpose.

My final project was quickly approaching, and our teacher had asked us to create our own Scarlet letter. I rushed home to surprise *Mamá Erito* with the news, and she immediately said, *la bordaremos* (we'll stitch the letter). We found the materials, created the pattern, tried out the style, and she began teaching me how to stitch the letter. She loved stories, and she asked me to tell her about Hester. So, I started piecing together bits of information I had gathered from the book, dictionary, and movie, along with some words I had picked out during class.

Every night, as I sat with her stitching the letter A, *Mamá Erito* would ask me what I thought of the book and how Hester might have felt about carrying the letter. She always added, *Ester era una mujer valiente* (Hester was a brave woman). Through this process, *Mamá Erito* not only taught me how to stitch, but she showed me her way of doing school. I was engaging with the book that once had caused so much anxiety. I felt safe and loved sitting at home with my *abuela*, doing needlework and talking. I was the only one in class who had beautifully stitched a large A. *La maestra* (The teacher) was very impressed with my work; she even asked if she could keep my A in her classroom as an example for other students.

While I encountered a difficult learning context at school because of my still-developing English skills, using Mamá Erito's knowledge to approach this text lowered my "affective filter" (Krashen, 1982) and allowed me to actively participate in the learning process. The fact that my teacher recognized the work invested in this project validated my learning journey.

At the microlevel, it is crucial to consider the following:

- As a teacher, how do my language practices invite every child into the learning process?
- How are languages represented and valued in my classroom?
- How do I recognize and celebrate the linguistic practices of the families in my classroom?

At the macrolevel, it is important to consider how language is used in the school:

- Is a hierarchical language structure present in your school, valuing certain languages over others?
- Are multiple ways of communicating (oral and written) available for families and students to ask questions as well as share knowledge?
- Are translations of official documents readily available?
- When using translations, is the language register accessible to all parents?

Question to Consider

- How often do you stop to think about whether key materials are accessible to all the families in your school?

LIVING THROUGH LANGUAGE: COMMUNITY AND SCHOOL

Let us now reflect on the role language plays in the migration process. Once families decide to leave what they know behind, the process of saying goodbye to loved ones, familiar places, sounds, scents, and colors begins. It becomes a combination of pain and hope, of great expectation and troubled uncertainty. Families are able to make sense of their emotions and actions through language (i.e., writing lists and goodbye notes, filling out paperwork, completing transactions at the bank, recording important contact numbers). Language is the tool that supports families in navigating this complex process.

Moving to the unknown is never a decision taken lightly. Often, one family member arrives first, leaving children, spouse, and parents behind. In certain cases, it takes decades before families can be reunited. Knowing the challenges of relocating to a new country, culturally and linguistically diverse (CLD) families generally move to towns/cities where a network has been already established (Boyd, 1989); that is, a family member or friend has previously migrated, set up connections, and established roots. Once housing has been found, families can begin to think toward finding a school. Yet, frequently there are innumerable other tasks that first must be completed in order to meet the basic needs of the family. Table 2.1 summarizes some of the actions CLD families generally take before

Table 2.1. Early Actions and Language Uses to Establish a Family in a New Community

Action	Language Uses
Find appropriate housing (e.g., renting or buying a home without credit history)	Complete a rental application, arrange a security deposit, provide letters of reference
Obtain identification documents	Navigate a particular government agency
Find work	Complete employment application, go through the interview process, complete any additional tasks required by the employer
Find health services (i.e., medical, dental, visual) and establish a health record for enrollment purposes	Locate the health department, complete paperwork, recover and send health records
Buy a car without credit history (if families have financial resources to purchase a vehicle)	Locate possible vehicles that match the family's needs, negotiate the terms of the purchase, secure insurance, and obtain a valid driver's license
Access phones or the Internet	Obtain documentation to acquire these services
Use public transportation	Navigate maps, schedules, and routes using posted signage, documents, or apps
Access a public library	Navigate the library system to obtain a library card and maximize use of the resources offered
Seek government assistance	Understand requirements, complete forms, navigate the nuances of these services

enrolling their children in school. Consider the role language plays for each.

Challenges for families when preparing for school include:

- Accessing paperwork needed to officially complete enrollment processes
- Understanding how the school system works
- Understanding how their documented or undocumented immigrant status may be a factor at school
- Buying school supplies
- Understanding the transportation system of the school

- Communicating with teachers and administrators
- Completing school forms (e.g., release forms)
- Accessing technology at home

In our attempt to prepare classrooms and lesson plans for incoming children, we often forget the preparation that is taking place by families and overlook how assistance may be needed to address the linguistic dimension in order to be ready for that first day of class. Beyond providing back-to-school supply lists, communication and support for families can be limited. Reaching out to families to determine what support might be needed is key to easing the transition for students and families.

The Hidden Work of Families: Understanding How to Navigate the School System

Registering children in school, making sure their shots are up to date, and buying school supplies may seem like programmed practices for every family with school-aged children at the beginning of each school year. It is assumed that families understand where to gain access to the needed items and how to successfully negotiate the process of registration. However, for CLD families, every single task involves jumping into the unknown, equipped with whatever tools may be available, and hoping for the best results. For example, when registering their children in school, new CLD families must understand the forms provided and be aware of the types of information requested by the school. Unfortunately, not every school's front office staff is equipped to guide families as they make sense of the information required in a language that is unfamiliar to them. It is not atypical to walk into a front office and see families sitting with their children trying to make sense of what is being asked of them—and children are often the ones filling out the forms.

When school employees do not reflect the cultural and linguistic diversity of their student population, schools must be committed to providing high-quality translation and interpretation services, ensuring the language used is both accessible and accurate. The surrounding community becomes the school's greatest asset. Developing a running list of language representatives who belong to the community and who are willing to volunteer can help create a more inviting atmosphere for incoming parents, and serve as an additional resource for parents trying to support students' learning at home. Often these partners include CLD parents who have created formal or informal networks to help new families become familiar with school processes. These language partners could also include partnerships with local businesses that encourage their workers to complete community service, or universities (i.e., professors, students, and student organizations) who are able to count this activity as service or for class credit.

Certain school districts are equipped with welcome centers. These centers are designed to support families as they enroll their children in school. Nonetheless, not every school district has the financial resources to offer this sort of holistic support. Additional resources do exist, such as translators at government agencies who are available to support new clients seeking information, such as medical records at the health department. Yet, knowing these resources are available also involves a navigation process. Needless to say, languaging is a skill ubiquitously required as new CLD families engage in what it means to "go to school" in the United States.

Families Don't Show Up

To better understand the power of language in the dynamic between schools and CLD families, we must pay attention to messages derived from common statements that are frequently shared. In this section of the chapter, we explore how perceptions of one another become entrenched in our mindset based on language used. For example, when parents are not yet accustomed to certain procedures, what assumptions are made by school staff? What types of generalizations form if parents do not attend school-sponsored functions? How do these assumptions and generalizations become shared sentiments?

The process of making meaning is interactional. As stated earlier, language can create liberating or oppressive learning spaces. When statements are shared among educators about a particular group of students or families, these statements foster a mindset that can lead to assumptions, generalizations, and even bias. Labeling theory (Becker, 1963) points to the danger inherent in using language to label individuals. This process can limit our ability to understand and appreciate the multiple facets of another individual due to the meaning associated with certain labels. Labels such as "at risk," "marginalized," or even "gifted" can frame the way individuals are treated and reinforce hegemonic power structures.

Questions to Consider

- How often do you stop to think about the language you use in the classroom?
- What terminology do you use that may create limiting or dichotomous ways of seeing?

In her early work on white privilege, Peggy McIntosh coined the phrase "unpacking the invisible knapsack" (McIntosh, 1989). She uses this phrase as a metaphor for challenging white privilege and recognizing social practices that systematically normalize and reinforce white culture. It is difficult to see how our perceptions may be rooted in national, socioeconomic, racial, linguistic, or cisgendered privilege. As individuals, we normalize what is familiar to us, especially if it is advantageous. Social practices become normalized by language used in official documents and policies but also in the daily thoughts, phrases, comments, and statements that describe our way of seeing the world and one another. Language plays a pivotal role in how perceptions, labels, and practices are either reified or dismantled. Consider the principal's words in the following scenario:

Principal Thompson's Confession

Principal Thompson has been a principal for 22 years. She has served in the same school district for 19 of those years. During that time, she has watched the demographics of the town where she lives and works change dramatically. Due to the number of industry and agricultural opportunities in the area, she has seen the school's population shift from a predominantly white and middle-class community to a CLD population. Principal Thompson has welcomed the change and has been a longtime advocate for multicultural education. With the change of her school's population, she has been devoted to offering staff development on issues surrounding cultural competency and makes conscientious efforts to have school signs, official written materials, and website resources in multiple languages. She feels that she and her staff have worked exceptionally hard at making the school a welcoming space. Despite such efforts, CLD family attendance has remained extremely low at parent conferences, school meetings, and social events organized by the school.

Reflecting on the issue of parent participation, she said, "We literally can't do any more than what we are doing to get our immigrant and minority families to be active participants. We have offered child care, food, rotating schedules, parent language academies, home visits, multicultural representations in our halls and classrooms, a committed staff, and an open-door policy for classroom and lunchtime visits. No matter what we offer, they just don't show up, regardless of what we do. I have the same traditional families show up without much representation of our nontraditional families. What are we supposed to do? Am I responsible for literally going to their home and bringing each family myself? Don't they know their child's success depends on them? What more can I do to convey this? At this point, I am about ready to give up and say, if they come, they come. But, I know deep down that isn't the right attitude."

> ## Questions to Consider
> - What emotion(s) are you sensing from this confession?
> - What are key words used in Principal Thompson's statement that need to be analyzed or "unpacked"?

Cultural differences that CLD families face in the process of "doing school" can be overwhelming. When these new procedures are combined with transportation and work schedules, attending school events becomes challenging. Schools across the nation have responded in various ways to help improve family attendance at organized gatherings. Some schools have offered transportation or ride programs while others have provided child care. Organizational shifts also have occurred to make meetings more inclusive by providing translators and incorporating cultural celebrations in school functions. Despite such attempts, school officials continue to share with us their disillusionment concerning low attendance among CLD families.

It is natural to feel discouraged after attempting to organize events to bring a school community together and then having the same few families show up each time. When this occurs repeatedly, perceptions begin to form about those not in attendance. In the case of Principal Thompson, you can sense both her commitment to families as well as her eventual acceptance of low CLD family attendance: "They just don't show up." The wording in Principal Thompson's statement reflects a school-centric mentality reliant on dichotomous words (we/they, [us]/them, traditional/nontraditional) that reinforce binary ways of seeing and approaching the issue of community and family engagement. Despite the multiple efforts by Thompson's staff to welcome families, the emphasis on "They" in describing who is not showing up generalizes and otherizes CLD families while creating bias against families not adhering to set expectations. Beyond thinking about dichotomous language, we as educators must also unpack what it means to "show up." Is attending a meeting or school function still the constant for defining what it means to "show up" in support of a child's learning?

Ways Families Do Show Up: Shifting Perceptions

In innumerable ways that often go overlooked, families show up for their children and communicate the value of an education. Families do the best they can, given their personal circumstances, to make sure their children are fed, attend school, complete their homework (even though parents may not be able to provide support due to the language of instruction), have clean clothes to wear, and feel loved. Families also show up by sustaining their transgenerational narratives. These narratives help children connect with their ancestors' histories, culture, and language. Conveying transgenerational narratives supports children's process of understanding who they are as individuals, and how to make sense of their new culture and language without feeling lost. Such narratives can be used as an instructional tool to inform and transform our curriculum on a daily basis. Table 2.2 provides ways teachers can make family biographies a part of instructional time. Curricular implications are explored further in Chapter 3 when we discuss the role of homework.

As teachers, we can create family participatory inventories highlighting the multiple ways in which families do show up for the students in our classrooms. Such practices may not always be congruent with how schools have envisioned parental engagement in the past. However, affirming the efforts and acknowledging the sacrifices families already make for the well-being and education of their children has the potential to powerfully enhance our students' school experience. By taking this step, we demonstrate to students and families that we value who they are and what they know.

Table 2.2. Curricular Applications of Family Biographies

Curriculum	Ways Teachers Can Draw from Family Narratives
Mathematics	Utilize family backgrounds to create and write word problems. Analyze the language used in the word problem to connect language and content instruction.
Language Arts and Social Studies	Accommodate schedules and transportation to facilitate the visit of a community elder in the classroom. Afterward, use the narrative to co-construct a big book with students. Analyze plot, setting, and characters in the context of the narrative that is familiar to students. Explore historical contexts and connections.
Science	Apply science concepts (e.g., measurement, sequencing, creating/following directions, plant life cycles) to a family's recipe, farming skills, or knowledge of traditional medicine/ the healing properties of plants. Analyze and discuss the language used in each science-related lesson.

Questions to Consider

- How much time do you spend with colleagues to create curriculum that incorporates real-world materials and transgenerational narratives?
- Are collaborations such as these a priority to your school?
- How might you advocate for time to work with colleagues on such projects?

Supporting Intrinsic and Extrinsic Steps

Improving family and community engagement begins with recognizing the power of language, particularly how it shapes our reality and frames our relationships with one another. The process of creating inclusive spaces begins with examining how language is used to describe and reinforce cultural norms, social practices, and perceptions based on our own experiences. It requires reflection and humility to unpack our own bias and recognize how fossilized practices may not be creating the liberating learning spaces we desire. Developing this intrinsic self-awareness is the most fundamental step in reducing barriers among the school, family, and community. Authentic conversations between each member of the school–family–community triad can lead to creative ways of working together and honoring the contributions of each partner in the child's learning and development.

Once educators commit to the active process of learning and unlearning, asking and listening, the structural, more extrinsic steps can be taken to help create pathways for growing attendance at school events. In Chapter 4, we discuss the importance of listening to the wishes of families when implementing such events. Often the first extrinsic change is creating events that are of interest to families, based on their expressed needs and wishes. Discovering what these needs and wishes are does not result from using a generic form or survey. Rather, this discovery process is reliant on interacting and investing time with the families served at the school, utilizing language as a tool for understanding. That being said, there are times throughout the course of the year when forms and mass communication are needed. Table 2.3 provides suggestions for addressing typical communication needs for schools.

Remember, however, that language is interactional. Schools are not the only partner in the triad attempting to address the obstacles CLD families face when navigating institutional procedures and expectations. New families, too, are continually enacting their own agency and striving to find ways to be involved in their children's education

Table 2.3. School-Based Communication Needs and Solutions

Communication Needs	Potential Solutions
Translation of Forms and Letters	The school creates an inventory of the languages represented by its students and attempts to find community members (e.g., in universities, colleges, faith-based organizations) who can help translate forms in ways that are accessible to families. Careful attention to the linguistic register used in these forms promotes understanding.
Registration	The school develops a registration fair in which community members who represent the languages of the school population are invited as volunteers to support families as they make sense of the registration process. Food and information on other useful services are provided during the event.
Transportation	The school identifies which families need transportation services and systematically creates a carpooling service to facilitate parents' access to meetings or school gatherings.

beyond the home. For instance, when language and transportation issues exist, they often find community members who are able to support them by translating, offering transportation, or filling out paperwork. The hidden work of families lies in identifying community members who are able to provide these kinds of services, establishing a relationship of mutual support with these individuals, coordinating schedules, and negotiating time off with employers.

CONCLUSION

We encourage communities and schools to reconceptualize their curriculum, analyze the language used in the classroom, and challenge former notions of what knowledge is and how it is interpreted, valued, and maximized. Part of this process involves the intrinsic work of unpacking assumptions derived from the language we use to describe the world, our communities, and one another. How can schools begin to shift historically entrenched practices that alienate families and communities based on us/them mentalities or negative perceptions of CLD families? This is precisely where the role of dialogue becomes paramount.

We must use language not only to promote but also to *listen*. We must begin this work by listening to students and families, followed by honoring the agency of each member of the school–family–community triad (this topic is explored in depth in Chapter 4). Once we are able to listen with a brave heart and recognize our limitations, we can begin to outline together the changes we desire in our communities and schools. Through listening sessions, we are able to identify creative ideas, community resources, and services that can be made accessible to the community-at-large (i.e., multiple venues/formats). The integration of these resources and services can be juxtaposed with our current curriculum and its learning standards to further a sense of congruency and collaboration between school and home.

These processes involve all stakeholders through constant communication and modification of how we approach learning, communicating, and teaching. The dialoguing and modifying creates a symbolic process of meaning making that is authentic to families and educators alike. Thus, learning standards are met using community resources and collective knowledge and language practices, and we become united in both mission and vision. Figure 2.1 provides a model of the interrelated components of community-based teaching.

Figure 2.1. Community-Based Teaching

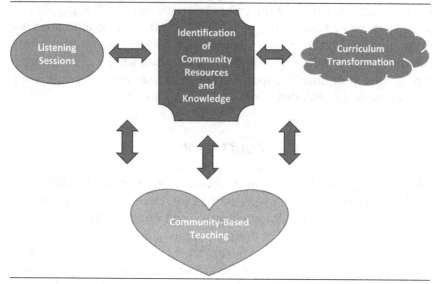

Check It Out
(Questions to Guide Reflection and Discussion)

1. Critically reflect on ways you have approached language in your classroom:
   - In what ways do you value students' linguistic diversity in the classroom?
   - Is it difficult to reflect on how you use language in the classroom? Why or why not? Describe a reflective process you could try.
   - List three ways you will begin to transform your curriculum to support more inclusive language practices.

Plan It Out
(Creating an Idea That Requires Action)

2. In a team, think and act on the following:
   - Devise a plan to identify key community members in your area.
   - Determine how you can create conversation spaces with community members to identify resources to use in your teaching.

Try It Out
(Attempting Action and Reflecting upon Outcomes)

3. Experiment with the following:
   - To begin creating conversation spaces, consider organizing listening sessions in various languages with families and community members to understand the challenges, needs, and wishes they have for strengthening home/school/community relations.
   - Create a process to safeguard the feedback.
   - Continue planning, using the feedback from the listening sessions.

Momentos de Reflexión (Moments of Reflection)

1. How will I counter the prevalent notion that CLD families "don't show up"?
2. How can I better demonstrate that I value the multiple ways CLD families participate?
3. In what ways will I transform my own linguistic practices to create more inclusive environments?

REFERENCES

Anzaldúa, G. (1981). Speaking in tongues: A letter to 3rd world women writers. In C. Moraga & G. Anzaldúa (Eds.), *This bridge called my back: Writings by radical women of color* (pp. 165–174). Watertown, MA: Perisphone Press.

Becker, H. (1963). *Outsiders: Studies in the sociology of deviance.* New York, NY: Free Press.

Boyd, M. (1989). Family and personal networks in international migration: Recent developments and new agendas. *International Migration Review, 23*(3), 638–670.

Carroll, J. B. (Ed.). (1956). *Language, thought, and reality: Selected writings of Benjamin Lee Whorf.* Cambridge, MA: MIT Press.

Herrera, S. G. (2016). *Biography-driven culturally responsive teaching* (2nd ed.). New York, NY: Teachers College Press.

Krashen, S. (1982). *Principles and practice in second language acquisition.* Oxford, UK: Pergamon Press.

McIntosh, P. (1989, July/August). White privilege: Unpacking the invisible knapsack. *Peace and Freedom Magazine,* 10–12.

Shohamy, E. (2006). *Language policy: Hidden agendas and new approaches.* New York, NY: Routledge.

Vygotsky, L. (1962). *Thought and language.* New York, NY: Wiley.

CHAPTER 3

Burying Fossilized Practices
Disrupting *los Deberes* (Homework)

Every home is a university and the parents are the teachers.

—Mahatma Gandhi

> **Key Concepts:** fossilized practices, *los deberes*, additive perspective, authentic *cariño*, *manualidades*

INTRODUCTION

Homework. *Deberes.* Central to many of the complexities surrounding the role parents play in the schooling of their children, homework seems to be ever present in what it means to be an engaged parent. For many teachers, support with homework completion *defines* what it means to be an involved and caring parent. Discourse themes that are heard in school lounges include: "These parents don't care. They aren't active participants in the education of their children. There is no sense in sending homework home—it never gets done." Lumped into these statements are notions about how often culturally and linguistically diverse (CLD) students are inconsistent in completing their homework, which leads to teachers wondering, "How can I be an effective teacher if these students have no support at home?"

Think about the following scenario and reflect on the way "care" and "support" of schooling is different based on the unique sociocultural dimension of the student's home.

Martha's Story

I had, as many of my family members often commented, crossed to the other side. Often leaving behind what I knew from my lived experiences, I was attempting to create a new template for how things should be. I was off to become a teacher. For many years, I had been away from my extended family, the family who valued education as much as the next person. After completing my degree in teaching, I only returned for short visits, as time permitted.

During my teacher preparation program, I never questioned the models presented to me on what role parents should play in their child's education. I was conditioned to the expectation—the "how to" instructions—for how parents become active participants in their child's learning. Within that training, I was conditioned to believe that parents were to encourage and support the child in completing homework, provide quiet spaces for this to occur, and communicate with the teacher at designated times (i.e., parent-teacher conferences). Good parents practiced spelling words, read to their children, completed science projects, and were attentive to making sure that what was sent home was then returned the next day with the task completed. Parents who did not do this were placed on the "need to work with these parents" list or dismissed as not caring about their child's future.

I bought into this narrative. I complied. I made sure to send home worksheets with letters, numbers, and shapes for students to practice with their parents. I sent books in Ziploc bags to be read with parents and the signature logs to keep up with the time spent reading. This was a weekly ritual. I was evaluated on complying with the unwritten district directive on homework. I was told these practices were good for families and kids. After all, this is what would lead to increased reading scores and to framing a love of reading.

I never questioned the Ziploc bags, the homework log, or any other take-home task my principal asked me to carry out; this was what I was trained to do. Never mind that the children and parents I was serving, like my own parents, did not have the English language, time (due to long workdays), or understanding to fully participate in what I was asking of them. I should have known better. However, I subscribed to this one-size-fits-all way of doing and thinking deeply embedded in the system we call school.

Fast forward 20 years. My mother was not doing well and I returned for an extended stay with my family. I stayed with my cousin Bertha for weeks at a time, so I was privy to the dynamics of what happened before and after school with her two elementary-school-aged boys. Bertha, a stay-at-home mom, was the unofficial community social worker, healer, driver, and liaison. She also served as the pivotal point of contact for our very large extended family, opening her home and heart when we most needed love, support, and attention. At the same time, she attended to her own family, running her home like a well-oiled machine.

I sat every morning and had a cup of coffee and homemade tortillas, gathering the energy to go back to the hospital, and returning in the evening to commiserate on the events of the day. I was amused with Bertha's daily routine of signing the homework log on one day and the reading log the next. I noticed that the reading log was placed in a Ziploc bag, along with the leveled book to be read that evening. The homework assignment came with a completion log, where students earned smiley faces toward prizes at the end of the month. Each week, I watched the same routine: The boys would return from school, help around the house, play games, eat dinner, take a bath, and go to bed. Each morning arrived with breakfast, Ziploc bags opened and logs signed, then out the door to school.

At the end of the first month, finding myself reflecting on how little the routine had changed, and how similar she was to my own mother in signing what was put before her, I asked: "Bertha, what is it that you sign every day for the boys?" She laughed a deep laugh and replied, "Yo no sé, no mas que no sea que les doy permiso que me saquen de aquí!" ("I don't know what I am giving permission to as long as it doesn't say they are removing me from here!") At that moment, I realized how incongruent our educational system was and continues to be when it comes to what we expect to take place at home. I had bought into the routine because it was what I was asked to do, knowing full well the families of my students did not hold my same perspective on our shared responsibility.

Questions to Consider

- What messages did you receive during your teacher preparation program?
- What is the purpose of homework in your current practice?
- In what ways do you consider the biography of the learner in assigning homework?
- Does the homework you assign look different from what was assigned when you were in school?
- Does the population you serve now look like the population of the classrooms you attended?

Today, homework is a contested topic among students, parents, teachers, administrators, and researchers (Carr, 2013). Most teachers continue to assign homework in outdated ways without asking what is best for the population they serve. For students at large, research indicates that homework can have a significant influence on achievement, yielding percentile gains between 8% and 13% (Van Voorhis, 2011). However, research also indicates that economically disadvantaged students are marginalized by ineffective homework practices (e.g., Bennet & Kalish, 2006; Kohn, 2006). Redding (2000) argues that homework, if implemented well, can have an impact on learning that is three times greater than the effect of socioeconomic status.

Given what has been learned from research, we as educators should be questioning: What constitutes effective homework? As part of this discussion, we need to consider the families we serve. How can we move toward contextualizing homework designed to not only contribute to student learning but also provide opportunities for parents, siblings, and extended family members to draw from their own wisdom and wealth of knowledge?

This chapter attempts to disrupt fixed or "fossilized" notions of homework in order to reconceptualize *los deberes* as a guide that promotes learning without further marginalizing families and CLD communities. By examining the history, attitudes, and alienating impact of homework for students and parents alike, we are able to re-envision its use. Readers are urged to define the construct of homework within their own practice, imagine the possibilities, and develop a plan of action for the future.

HOMEWORK AS A FOSSILIZED PRACTICE

Fossils serve as artifacts that explain historical evolutions over time. Yet the fossil itself has cycled through its life stages and remains in its final form: fixed, rigid, and ossified. We use the term *fossilized* to symbolically critique current practices within education that are fixed, rigid, and ossified, hindering the evolving nature of the communities they are intended to serve.

One of the most significant examples of fossilization in instructional practices is evident when we analyze the meaning and use of homework. Dr. Harris Cooper has conducted research on the subject of homework for decades and has published multiple texts on the subject. In one of his earlier publications, he defined homework as any task "assigned to students by school teachers that are meant to be carried out during non-school hours" (Cooper, 1989, p. 7). Cooper later amended this definition, changing "non-school hours" to "non-instructional time," because homework is sometimes completed during study hall or during the course of the day (Bembenutty, 2011). Despite this modification of the definition to incorporate *when* homework is being completed, critical analysis of *what* is being assigned as homework and *why* it is being assigned is lacking.

Homework generally is limited in scope and typically encompasses worksheets, spelling lists, maps to be colored, math computation, or timed math tests. Each of these examples has remained unchanged for decades. How many times have you heard someone say, "I remember doing these worksheets when I was a kid"? Whether this statement is meant to be humorous, nostalgic, or an attempt to commiserate with the child completing the task, we must critically examine why we continue to approach homework in this way.

Think about the following vignette. Does this family's struggle resonate with the type of homework that is part of today's schooling routine?

The Monday Packet

The routine is always the same at the Sanchez household. The homework packet (see example in Figure 3.1) arrives on Monday. Each week there are pages filled with mind-numbing, fill-in-the-blank worksheets intended to teach phonics, word definitions, and spelling. For the Sanchez family, the

Figure 3.1. Traditional Spelling Packet

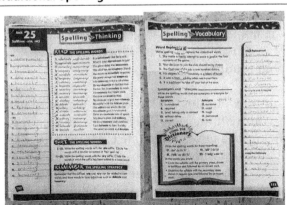

battle is real. Sofia, an above-average student in school, avoids completion of the assignment packet for a variety of reasons. First, phonics always has been difficult, given that her first language is not English. Although she routinely scores 100% on the spelling test on Friday, she struggles to complete the fill-in-the blank portion of the packet. Her parents feel helpless in supporting her with the work. Both have college degrees from their home county but do not speak English. Both hate seeing the sadness in Sofia's eyes as she attempts to do the work and becomes frustrated. For the family and Sofia, there seems to be no alternative, so they make the decision to not have Sofia do the work.

Questions to Consider

• Does the type of assignment in Figure 3.1 look familiar?
• In what ways could spelling homework be more authentic?

Fossilized homework practices are a perfect example of good intentions gone awry. We all want to support students' ongoing development. However, we need to remember that *love of learning* is the motivation that drives forward progress!

The following questions regarding homework can help us to evaluate our own usage of homework.

• Does homework assigned inspire students to take their classroom learning to the next level, with applications to their own lives?
• Does the homework invite students to learn from those who hold places of greatest love, authority, and power in their lives (e.g., parents, caregivers, extended family members)?
• Does the homework encourage self-reflection and creativity, both of which are sometimes difficult to build into our busy classroom routines?

The goal throughout this book is for the reader to have an honest conversation with self, and with colleagues, about practices such as homework that need a new spirit of life breathed into them—practices that support building positive relationships between students and their families, and between families and the classroom. Our objective is to get to the root of obstacles that inhibit our abilities as educators to support our students' academic, linguistic, and emotional development.

The next section of this chapter addresses public sentiment and reactive tendencies for or against homework. It also proposes how we might begin to transform the meaning of homework and its usage.

FROM PENDULUM SWINGS TO PARADIGM SHIFTS: DISRUPTING *LOS DEBERES*

Despite its format remaining unchanged, sentiments on the concept of homework have varied greatly over the years. Much like a pendulum swinging back and forth, viewpoints on homework have reflected extreme shifts over time, and these shifts often have been influenced by economic competition or political tensions. In his book, *The Battle over Homework*, Harris Cooper (2006) analyzes public sentiment toward homework throughout history. He claims, "Homework controversies have followed a thirty-year cycle with public outcries for more or less homework every fifteen years apart." He provides various examples, such as the general public's push for more rigor in homework during the Cold War. The goal during that time was for U.S. students to advance in math and science. This sentiment shifted in the late 1960s in favor of decreasing homework, due to excessive amounts being assigned that were causing high levels of student stress. The pendulum shifted again toward increasing levels of homework in the late 1980s and 1990s as a result of the *Nation at Risk* report, followed by public sentiment at the turn of the century desiring reduced homework loads, due to student burnout and fatigue experienced by families as well as teachers (Cooper, 2006, p. 3).

A moderate approach to homework in recent decades, amid these pendulum swings, has been the "10-minute rule." Supported by the NEA and PTA, this approach to homework suggests that a daily maximum of 10 minutes of homework be assigned for each grade level completed. Therefore, a 3rd-grader shouldn't be expected to receive more than 30 minutes of homework per day.

Various scholars have argued that homework in moderation allows students extra time to practice skills that appear on standardized assessments while instilling a homework routine that helps students when they enter high school and college (Bempechat, 2004; Cooper, 2006; Eren & Henderson, 2011). Yet, as instructional time continues to increase by extending the school year, eliminating recess, or reducing lunch breaks, a growing number of school districts are deciding to ban homework, particularly at the elementary level. Proponents of this move argue that homework has not been correlated directly with learning gains or improving test scores, and they claim it is harming students' enthusiasm for learning while stunting their socioemotional development (Hirsh-Pasek, Golinkoff, & Eyer, 2004; Kralovec & Buell, 2001; Vatterott, 2009).

As homework increases, time for extracurricular activities, play, and family decreases. For students who spend considerable time working to help support the family, taking care of siblings, or getting dinner ready for the family, there is little time to devote to homework. These and many other circumstances often impede the student's ability to complete assigned work.

Differing perspectives on homework are reflected not only within educational literature and public sentiment, but also among educators themselves. Teachers within the same school often have polarizing views on the subject. Think about the following scenario. Where would you stand?

Solving the Homework Problem

The faculty were from a large urban high school in the Northeast that had a high English learner population. Several of the teachers at the school saw homework as an added stress to their students' demanding work and family schedules. They argued that there was absolutely no time for students to do homework. Others in the school claimed that abolishing homework was setting students up for failure by not setting high expectations. One teacher's solution was simply to tell the students to complete their homework while riding the bus home each afternoon.

Most educators, parents, and students likely would agree that a school bus is not a conducive site for completing homework. However, these are the sorts of conversations occurring both inside and outside schools across the country. What if the debate shifted from whether or not to assign homework, to redefining homework itself?

Questions to Consider

- When does homework cross the line to become an unacceptable stressor for students and teachers?
- In what ways are traditional methods of homework ineffective?
- How can homework responsively address the cultural and linguistic needs of our students?

To this point, we've problematized how the concept of homework has not changed in decades and how it continues to be a contested concept. The remaining portion of the chapter will address what we mean by "Disrupting los Deberes." The noun *el deber* in English means a duty or obligation. It is a word that implies action and often signifies an ongoing commitment. *Los deberes*, the term most often used in Spanish for homework, is something that you do and it is never passive. Yet, somehow, the majority of homework assigned in today's schools relies on the student's rote learning (e.g., through worksheets), with little connectivity to another individual or opportunities to situate learning within his or her own life. How do we re-envision homework to emphasize action-oriented learning? How can the relevance of homework be enhanced through cultural contextualization?

RE-ENVISIONING *LOS DEBERES*

To begin to re-envision *los deberes*, it is important to look at homework from an additive perspective. We do not mean "additive" in the sense of increasing more work. Rather, teachers must first ask, "What could be gained from this activity that would enhance *my* understanding of students?" *Los deberes* is just as much about the duty/investment of the teacher as it is about the students.

In its best version, homework tends to be a tool to assess what students understand or don't. Unfortunately, it is often a habitual task that feels like busy work and simply replicates class instruction. If students are overwhelmed by either the academic content being assessed or their outside extracurricular, family, or employment responsibilities, such homework is going to do little to enhance learning. The pervasive implementation of homework today does not afford teachers opportunities to understand or connect with their students. Rather, the focus remains on the final product, either by checking for completion or by assigning a letter grade with little emphasis on the process.

Homework alienates not only students but also families and caregivers. When re-envisioning *los deberes*, homework becomes an additive opportunity for teachers to learn about students and their families, as well as their cultural and experiential knowledge—knowledge they've gained through informal education outside the classroom. It is imperative, however, to examine how homework has been articulated to families. Part of the reflective practice required to disrupt *los deberes* is to perceive parents/caregivers as resources.

Families often have little knowledge about the learning taking place at school. If given updates, they are usually newsletters that summarize instructional units, brought home in *carpetas* (folders) or crumpled in student backpacks, often after the subject matter has been taught. Alternatively, updates are provided for parents through online platforms where they can view student performance. Yet this mode of communication is inaccessible to many families due to technological, linguistic, and/or economic differences. Both methods of communication surrounding homework are reactionary (occurring after the fact) and passive (with little to no interaction).

When teachers discuss homework directly with parents, the conversation often focuses on whether the child is doing the homework or not. To ensure it has been completed, parents often are required to sign documentation on a daily basis, especially for younger students. Yet the purpose of the assignment frequently remains unclear. Parents and caregivers, including those who reflect the dominant culture (white, middle-class, fluent in English, and formally educated), have little understanding for how to help their children in meaningful ways with assignments. As a result, much like teachers and students, parents/caregivers often end up going through the motions of homework. For parents, this means repetitively asking if students have homework, pushing them to do it, and signing off when it is completed, because that is what has always been done.

For CLD families, homework becomes an even more daunting undertaking. Often parents have to bridge both language and content in order to help their children understand the classroom demands. Homework seems to be so far removed from the learners' and families' experiences that it causes high levels of anxiety and creates a dissonant learning experience for students. Consider the following questions:

- How might *los deberes* offer a transformative perspective—one in which we can envision CLD families taking ownership and agency to foster successful learning environments for their children?
- In what ways might *los deberes* create optimal spaces for families and schools to work together in order to enact culturally and linguistically responsive teaching practices?

The goal of disrupting *los deberes* is finding ways to engage teachers, students, and families in the process of learning through respecting and utilizing community assets. The robotic act of homework situated and enacted away from the context of family and community must be eliminated in order to entertain the concept of disrupting *los deberes*. What if homework became the very tool to promote parental engagement? *Los deberes*, if reconceptualized (see examples in Table 3.1), has the ability to serve as a bridge between schools and family communities. In its fossilized form, however, it continues to remain a barrier.

Innovation Artifact: Finding New Ways to Engage Students and Families with Homework

---

Teachers who care about making caregivers part of the learning community are innovative in their approach to creating opportunities where all families can contribute to classroom learning. Such teachers plan for and assign homework that provides multiple entry points, making engagement possible for everyone, regardless of language, socioeconomic status, or educational background. They build the structure—the bridge—for valuing every voice and contribution. Through the journey they learn about families' funds of knowledge (Moll, Amanti, Neff, & González, 1992). Students begin to see themselves as equal members of the community of learners. In this way, classrooms become equitable spaces for teaching and learning.

Ms. Brown provides one example of the homework she utilizes with her students. She made the decision to forgo the traditional vocabulary assignment she had used for many years. Instead, she started using the linking language strategy (Herrera, Kavimandan, Perez, & Wessels, 2017) to activate students' prior knowledge and then build background, draw connections, and bring multiple perspectives into the lesson. She gave all students, regardless of language proficiency or academic level, the opportunity to share during the lesson.

Given the success she was having in the classroom, she made the decision to send the text-related pictures home and encourage parents/caregivers to engage with their children in conversation about them (see Figure 3.2 for letters sent home in English and in Spanish). The pictures they discussed were the same visuals Ms. Brown would be using for the lesson. This step provided students with an opportunity to maximize family resources as they began building from the known (family-sourced cultural and language connections) to the new content-area concepts and academic English language.

The results were powerful not only for students' academic and linguistic development, but also for Ms. Brown's building and solidifying relationships with her students' families. Letting go of tradition can be difficult, but the results are well worth the risk! Figure 3.3 provides artifacts from the activity and lesson progression.

Table 3.1. Re-envisioning Homework: Culturally Responsive Pathways for Bridging Home to School

Our homework assignments are only limited by prescribed ways of thinking. Moving forward will require knowledge of the biography of the learner—his or her home life, aspirations, and dreams. It will require discovering the community wealth and assets that lie outside our schools and that can inform learning in our content area. Think creatively and become innovative about gathering input from home to inform what you do in the classroom, while at the same time supporting students to consider new applications of content to the larger world.

SECONDARY LEVEL—Connecting to the Home and Community

	Content Area	Science
1	Biology, Chemistry, Physics	Learn about the community: Where are parents/caregivers or family members employed? Are there poultry farms, dairies, or other plants where caregivers or family members experience physics, chemistry, and biology on a daily basis? Send home questions and surveys to gather information that can be used to bridge between the science curriculum and students' lives. Use real-life examples to increase relevance and promote connections to background knowledge.
2	Botany, Earth Science	Learn about how different cultures interact with their surroundings. How are plants viewed culturally within different communities? Learn what health and food uses they may have within each home. Create homework assignments that allow students to share their knowledge and that increase vocabulary and conceptual knowledge for all learners.

		English
1	Literature	Have students explore the readings that their families are most familiar with from home, community, and school. Compare characters, traits, plot, and other literature concepts. How do they differ from culture to culture? In what ways are they the same?
2	English	Have students work with their families to find cognates (words that share the same meaning in two languages). Have students think about spelling, meaning, and the origins of words.

		Mathematics
1	Algebra, Geometry	At the beginning of the year, make a list of common jobs or daily activities that are aligned with real-life mathematical constructs. As you introduce content, have students discuss how algebra, essential math, geometry, or other concepts are practiced in their family's everyday life. For example: If the student has family (or personal) experience with construction, links can be made to algebra and geometry skills used in the framing of a house.

Social Studies

1	History, Geography	Have students list the countries, states, cities, or towns they have been in and the mode of transportation they took on their vacation(s), their move to the community, or their journey to the United States. Using a mind map, ask that they "splash" as many pictures and words as they can recall about rivers, landforms, borders, and so forth. Bank these and use to promote concept and skill development according to Social Studies standards.

ELEMENTARY SCHOOL—Connecting to the Home and Community

Reading

Content Area		
1	K–3	Have parents/caregivers or family members work with their students to find nursery rhymes, songs, and stories that align with the topic or content of the week. Have the students or parents/caregivers or family members share with the class.
2	4–6	Send the essential question of the week or theme of the unit home, and ask parents/caregivers or family members to gather pictures, draw, or write any connections they have to the topic of the week, essential question, or theme. Highlight connections during instruction throughout the week.

Mathematics

1	K–3	Have parents/caregivers or family members send pictures or familiar objects to introduce shapes, numbers, colors, and other mathematical concepts.
2	4–6	Have parents/caregivers or family members share with their children how they use math within their work or daily life experiences. In what ways do they use measurement, addition, subtraction, multiplication, division, algebra, and geometry? Provide opportunities for students to share what they learned with their peers.

Social Studies

1	K–3	Send home the theme or concepts students are learning. Prepare the students to ask questions of their families and bring back what they learned. Use the information to bridge into the curricular concepts and skills you are teaching.
2	4–6	Use technology to translate key pieces of the text into the native language of the learner. Have the student discuss with parents/caregivers or family members connections between the text and the essential question, topic, theme, or concepts of the unit. Bridge between what students share about their discussion and the objectives/activities of the lesson.

Figure 3.2. Homework Letter to Parents

Dear Family,

Attached you will find four pictures. These pictures connect to vocabulary we are studying this week at school. In order for your student to really understand a word, it is important for them to make connections to that word. That is where you can help! As part of their homework each week, I will send home vocabulary pictures for them to discuss with you. You do NOT have to do each picture but may if you would like. It also does NOT need to be done in 1 day. Here is an idea of how you can help.

Monday—Pick 1 or 2 pictures and discuss with your child what is happening in that picture. Help them write down a few words next to the picture to describe the picture. If the picture makes you think of something personally or reminds you of a story, please share that with your child. If you speak a language other than English at home, your child may write words in that language also. Next to them, I would like your child to write the English words, if possible.

Tuesday—Pick different pictures and do the same thing with them.

Wednesday—Your child will have the eight vocabulary words for the week listed in their AVID Binder (in class we call the binder BOB). Work with your child to match the word with the correct picture. Please discuss with your child why a word would connect to that picture. Your child should write the vocabulary word next to the picture. Again, if you would like, they may write the word in both English and your native language. This will help them connect with that word.

Thursday—Discuss a definition for the vocabulary words of the week. You do NOT have to do each picture/word, but please write the definition(s) for at least one picture on a separate page. Your child will hand in the attached picture page and the definition(s) page on Fridays.

I understand how important family is in a student's success in the classroom. I, too, look forward to learning from you!

I greatly appreciate your helping your student with this homework.

Ms. Brown

Estimada Familia:

Adjunto encontrará cuatro imágenes. Estas imágenes se conectan con el vocabulario que estamos estudiando esta semana en la escuela. Para que su niño(a) pueda entender con claridad una palabra, es importante que ellos(as) puedan conectarse a través de sus experiencias con esta palabra. ¡Allí es donde nos puede ayudar! Como parte de la tarea cada semana, enviaré a casa las imágenes de vocabulario para que sean discutidas en familia. Usted no tiene que escribir nada en los cuadros, pero si lo desea, lo puede hacer. No se tiene que terminar la tarea en un día. En el siguiente párrafo encontrará algunas ideas acerca de como usted puede apoyar a su niño(a).

lunes—Escoja 1 o 2 de las imágenes y discuta con su hijo(a) lo que sucede en la imagen. Ayúdelo(a) a escribir algunas palabras al lado de la imagen para poder describirla. Si la imagen Trae a su mente alguna historia personal, por favor, compártala con su hijo(a). Si usted habla algún otro idioma que no sea inglés en casa, sus hijos(as) también pueden escribir las palabras en ese idioma. Si es posible, pueden escribir las palabras en ambos idiomas (una al lado de la otra).

martes—Elija imágenes distintas y siga los mismos pasos.

miércoles—Su hijo(a) ya tendrá las ocho palabras del vocabulario para la semana que aparecen en su cuaderno AVID (en la clase lo llamamos el cuaderno BOB). Trabaje con su hijo(a) para que la palabra coincida con la imagen correcta. Por favor, converse con ellos acerca de la razón por la cual esta palabra tiene este significado en particular y como se relaciona a la imagen que están analizando. Su hijo(a) debe de escribir la palabra del vocabulario al lado de la imagen. Una vez más, si usted lo desea, puede escribir la palabra en inglés y en el idioma que usa en casa. Esto ayudará al niño(a) a encontrar más conexiones.

jueves—Converse con su niño(a) acerca de las definiciones de las palabras del vocabulario de la semana. Usted no tiene que trabajar con cada imagen o palabra, pero se recomienda que escoja al menos una palabra y escriba las definiciones en una página separada. Su hijo(a) entregará la página de imágenes y la pagina de las definiciones los viernes. La labor familia es sumamente importante en el éxito de nuestros niños en la escuela. ¡Yo también espero aprender mucho de su familia!

Le agradezco infinitamente su apoyo.
Ms. Brown

Figure 3.2. Homework Letter to Parents (continued)

TRANSFORMATIVE PEDAGOGICAL PRACTICES: FOSTERING RELATIONS BETWEEN TEACHERS AND CLD FAMILIES

Ideally, *los deberes* speaks to both students and families' cultural, academic, and linguistic assets while attempting to access the academic content in equitable and inclusive ways. For this to occur, educators must first understand and embrace the lives and experiences of the families they serve. CLD families feature a plethora of values, practices, and traditions. As these families make sense of their lives as they occur within the context of a new culture and language, they strive to negotiate their multifaceted identities in order to continue their family legacy.

Educators who are prepared and willing to recognize CLD families' narratives as legitimate and significant sources of knowledge must adopt transformational pedagogical practices. These practices encourage teachers to deeply reflect on their assumptions and genuinely

Figure 3.3. Using Linking Language to Gather Family Knowledge

In this homework sample, both the student and the parent added words in English related to the images.

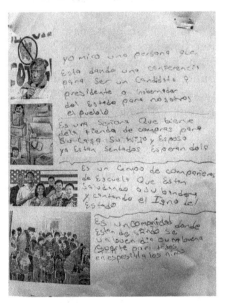

In this sample, the student responded to the images using the native language, Spanish.

English Translation:

Image 1: I look at a person who is giving a lecture to be a candidate for president or governor of the state for us the people.

Image 2: She is a lady who comes from the shopping store to her house; her son and husband are already sitting waiting for her.

Image 3: It is a group of schoolmates who are waving their flag and singing the state anthem.

Image 4: It is a community where they are wishing a good day and good luck for everyone, especially children.

Figure 3.3. Using Linking Language to Gather Family Knowledge *(continued)*

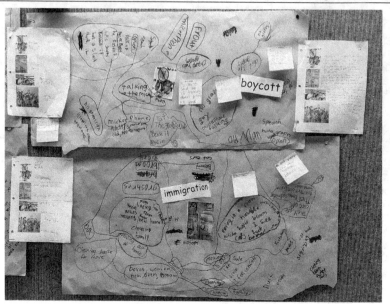

Pictured above are student products from the teachers' first phase of linking language strategy implementation. Having already discussed the images with their families through Ms. Brown's homework assignment, students were prepared to document connections to their background knowledge in writing. They discussed these personal connections in small groups. Then as a small-group team, they linked similar ideas and shared commonalties with the whole class.

Next, the teacher bridged to the lesson's content by having students decide which vocabulary words (e.g., boycott, immigration) matched best with which posters. Throughout the lesson, Ms. Brown continued to use students' words and ideas documented on the linking language posters to support their understanding of the academic content. By building from what students already knew, she thereby increased the relevance of the curriculum, supported their enduring understanding, and valued the life history of each individual in her learning community.

---

undertake a reciprocal teaching and learning model. In this model, families and educators are co-constructing knowledge by designing equitable and inclusive teaching and learning spaces rooted in the concept of authentic *cariño* (caring love).

Based on Noddings's (2002) philosophy of care, authentic *cariño* encourages teachers to be vulnerable and share the joys and sorrows encountered in the stories of the families they serve. Authentic *cariño* asks teachers to engage in a constant process of self-reflection and transformation to break down cultural, linguistic, and emotional barriers in order to build connections and trust. In addition, it urges teachers to adopt an active role of advocacy in supporting CLD families as they make sense of new educational environments, which often tend to be unfamiliar or even hostile.

Teachers, who cultivate authentic *cariño*, should strive to critically and humbly reflect on, transform, and adapt their pedagogies to generate a culture of encounter and kinship in the classroom among teachers, students, and families (Boyle, 2017). This process of understanding and supporting students' sociocultural, cognitive, linguistic, and academic growth (i.e., biographical literacy) (Herrera, Perez, & Escamilla, 2015) encourages teachers to embrace the vulnerability experienced by CLD families, and it inspires them to re-envision practices of kinship, compassion, and compatibility as together they rebuild a sustainable classroom ecology.

As educators make sense of the process of authentic *cariño* in the classroom, the following questions should be raised.

- How do I show authentic love for students and their families?
- Who are the CLD families being served? What are their narratives, stories, and biographies?
- What can schools learn from parents/caregivers and their communities?
- How can the wealth of family and community knowledge and experiences be incorporated in curricula that position students and their families at the center of the learning transaction?

Teachers who embrace the concept of transformational pedagogical practices through a lens of authentic *cariño* find tangible and meaningful ways to incorporate CLD families' experiences in their curriculum. The following sections provide a small sampling of ideas.

Honoring *la Novela Familiar*

CLD families' narratives can be conceptualized as honoring *la novela familiar*. Within the umbrella of CLD families, Latino/Latinx families will be used as an example to illustrate and further explore the concept of *la novela familiar*. Every night, in households across the nation, millions of families gather to watch how *la novela* unfolds. Families congregate in front of the television to laugh and cry about the fortunes and misfortunes of unusual protagonists and antagonists. Every night, *la familia* gathers to share stories, recount previous episodes, and predict what will occur next. In an intimate space, *la novela* creates opportunities to explore abstract concepts in literature such as the central theme, character development, settings, and multidimensional plots. These narratives often mirror the narratives of CLD families, in that they feature intricate stories of hope, loss, displacement, and belonging.

Tapping into *la novela familiar,* teachers could scaffold complex concepts in language arts, such as character development, opinions versus facts, main idea, inferences, plot structure, and setting. When teachers enter into conversations about the *novelas* their students are watching, they also can make comparisons to curricular texts. Teachers and students could participate in a comparative analysis identifying common themes in *la novela* and more traditional forms of literature. While incorporating the narrative of *la novela* could be a powerful tool in the classroom, teachers must recognize the problematic nature of how issues of equity, identity, race, and class are often represented in the storyline (Ronsini, 2009; Shohamy, 2006). Instead of avoiding these issues altogether, teachers could use *la novela* to address these topics in meaningful, instructional ways, such as by drawing parallels to the many life conflicts we all experience, ways family or friends serve as sources of strength, and that not all novels/stories have happy endings.

Integrating *Manualidades*

Schools should be equipped to discover the resources CLD families bring to the classroom. In a culturally and linguistically responsive learning environment, it is vital for teachers, staff, and administrators to use these resources as foundational support while reaching out to students and families. During intake sessions, when a new English learner arrives at the school, comprehensive information about the student's schooling is typically collected in order to identify the appropriate level of support. More often than not, this meeting necessitates a language and cultural liaison.

At this point, using an additive perspective, preliminary information about the child's family history could also be gathered—as long as the family is willing to share. School staff and teachers can use this first meeting to begin developing a relationship of trust with the family, which would evolve and grow throughout the year. The data gathered as this relationship develops could be used to create a detailed inventory of the family's cultural and linguistic resources or *manualidades*, the cultural and skill-based activities reflecting the talents, traditions, and interests of parents.

For instance, if the family identifies cooking, gardening, storytelling, writing, singing, and dancing as potential skills to be shared with the school, then these skills might be tapped in homework assignments as well as for school programs featuring these skills within and beyond the school boundaries to enhance cultural awareness, connection, compatibility, and community involvement. This shift requires purposeful planning, strategizing, and alignment at the district (e.g., ESOL office), school, and community levels. Using professional learning communities (PLCs) (Croft, Coggshall, Dolan, Powers, & Killion, 2010), teachers can find meaningful ways to incorporate these skills into their curricula, and administrators can encourage flexibility in district policies and mandates in order to open up spaces for these changes to occur.

Insights gathered through encounters with families and the community then inform dynamic classroom lessons and homework assignments that capitalize on CLD family resources. For instance, a cooking lesson could lead to a discussion of importing and exporting goods, with homework assignments to discuss what families know about conditions and locales for successfully growing specific products. Families also might have knowledge of chemicals used for growing and enhancing the quality of produce, transportation modes and routes of particular produce, and/or the sociocultural history of a particular product (e.g., spices, potatoes, rice). A gardening lesson could lead to making connections with biology or botany, mathematical measurements, or hydroponics, with homework tapping family knowledge about watershed systems, abundance and scarcity, variation from season to season and year to year, and water distribution. Storytelling, something that occurs within all families, could be incorporated in language arts homework to scaffold all four language skills: reading, listening, speaking, and writing (see McLaughlin & McLeod, 1996).

CONCLUSION

From reading packets and assigned books sent home in Ziploc bags to endless calculus problems that are expected to be completed on the bus ride home, our mindset and practices surrounding homework have become fossilized. Rather than focusing the conversation on whether or not to continue assigning homework, it is time to disrupt the concept of *los deberes* by re-envisioning how it can become a process that motivates and supports student learning while inviting family wisdom into the process. How might geography homework reflect the journeys of families instead of photocopied maps needing to be colored for each new unit? How can the *manualidades* of families be seen and used as assets in the learning process?

Homework that has been carefully designed and authenticated to meet the needs of students and allow for meaningful family support is effective for all. It is time to enhance the *quality* of homework, not the quantity. The potential benefits are limitless and include enhanced relationships based on *cariño* between teachers, students, and families, and particularly with CLD families who in the past have been excluded and shamed for not being "involved" in their children's education.

In many districts, schools, and classrooms across the country, the idea of flipping the classroom to provide more access to students and their families has grown as a method to not only provide classroom instruction, but also to think about homework through a different lens. A caution to this new way of thinking is that as educators, we forget to ask the relevant question related to what flipped classrooms mean on the receiving end. Many of our young adults work after school; parents/caregivers also may have many responsibilities that prevent them from participating in the flipped classroom. Families' access to technology and the literacy skills necessary to become full participants all need to be explored. At the end of the day, a well-conceived plan for grounding the flipped classroom in the potential, language, and cultural assets must be explored.

Chapter 4 will continue to examine fixed practices within K–12 schooling and the exclusion of CLD families by problematizing notions of school–family–community. The chapter highlights how school spaces are shared but never neutral, and how priority often is given to parents who are White, who have access to financial resources, and who are fluent in English. The chapter analyzes how such practices create divided spaces and closed school cultures that cause parents to feel alienated and become excluded. As part of this chapter, we examine the need to involve all caregivers (e.g., neighbors, mentors, leaders within community) as part of parental engagement, and how this expanded idea of community has an impact on learning. By building on community assets and establishing ongoing exchanges, students gain cultural context to their language learning and are motivated to serve as change agents within their communities.

Check It Out
(Questions to Guide Reflection and Discussion)

---

1. Critically reflect on the ways you have approached homework:
   - Why has the format of homework not changed over the years? How can homework reflect the cultural and linguistic practices of your students and their families?
   - What types of resources do you have available in order to make homework a more dynamic and meaningful endeavor?
   - What does the term *accessible* mean to you? How have you attempted to make yourself, your curriculum, and your classroom more accessible to CLD families?

Plan It Out
(Creating an Idea That Requires Action)

---

2. In a team, think and act on the following:
   - Find tangible ways to create university/community partnerships to support families' linguistic and cultural needs.
   - Design a sustainable method to gather information from CLD families.
   - Devise a plan for how you can reach out to families throughout the school year to show you care.

Try It Out
(Attempting Action and Reflecting upon Outcomes)

---

3. Act and reflect through the following:
   - Implement at least one element of your plans to learn more information about the families you serve. What did you learn?
   - In addition to transforming homework to better utilize family knowledge, how might you incorporate changes into your daily curriculum, based on your new insights?
   - In what ways can you hold yourself accountable toward being consistent with changes in your pedagogical practices?
   - How will you receive feedback from your students and CLD families on the effectiveness of your transformative pedagogy?

Momentos de Reflexión (Moments of Reflection)

1. In what ways am I willing to commit to reconceptualizing my usage of homework?
2. How can I better listen with authentic *cariño* during my revisioning of homework to hear the ideas of students and parents?
3. In what ways will I advocate for redefining what it means to do homework with the students and families I serve?

REFERENCES

Bembenutty, H. (2011). The last word: An interview with Harris Cooper—research, policies, tips, and current perspectives on homework. *Journal of Advanced Academics, 22*(2), 340–350.

Bempechat, J. (2004). The motivational benefits of homework: A socio-cognitive perspective. *Theory into Practice, 43*(3), 189–196.

Bennet, S., & Kalish, N. (2006). *The case against homework: How homework is hurting children and what parents can do about it.* New York: Penguin Random House.

Boyle, G. (2017). *Barking to the choir: The power of radical kinship.* New York: Simon & Schuster.

Carr, N. S. (2013). Increasing the effectiveness of homework for all learners in an inclusive classroom. *School Community Journal, 23*(1), 169–182.

Cooper, H. (1989). *Homework.* White Plains, NY: Longman.

Cooper, H. (2006). *The battle for homework: Common ground for administrators, parents and teachers.* Thousand Oaks, CA: Corwin Press.

Croft, A., Coggshall, J., Dolan, M., Powers, E., & Killion, J. (2010). *Job-embedded professional development: What it is, who is responsible, and how to get it done well.* National Comprehensive Center for Teacher Quality, Mid-Atlantic Comprehensive Center, and the National Staff Development Council.

Eren, O., & Henderson, D. (2011). Are we wasting our children's time by giving them more homework? *Economics of Education Review, 30*(5), 950–961.

Herrera, S. G., Kavimandan, S. K., Perez, D. R., & Wessels, S. (2017). *Accelerating literacy for diverse learners: Classroom strategies that integrate social/emotional engagement and academic achievement, K–8* (2nd ed.). New York, NY: Teachers College Press.

Herrera, S. G., Perez, D. R., & Escamilla, K. (2015). *Teaching reading to English language learners: Differentiating literacies.* Boston, MA: Pearson.

Hirsh-Pasek, K., Golinkoff, R., & Eyer, D. (2004). *Einstein never used flashcards.* New York, NY: Rodale.

Kohn, A. (2006). *The homework myth: Why our kids get too much of a bad thing.* Boston, MA: Capo Press.

Kralovec, E., & Buell, J. (2001). *The end of homework: How homework disrupts families, overburdens children, and limits learning.* Boston, MA: Beacon Press.

McLaughlin, B., & McLeod, B. (1996). *Educating all our children from culturally and linguistically diverse backgrounds.* Impact statement/final report on the accomplishments of the National Center for Research on Cultural Diversity and Second Language Learning, submitted to the U.S. Department of Education.

Moll, L. C., Amanti, C., Neff, D., & González, N. (1992). Funds of knowledge for teaching: Using a qualitative approach to connect homes and classrooms. *Theory into Practice, 31*(2), 132–141.

Noddings, N. (2002). *Starting at home: Caring and social policy.* Oakland, CA: University of California Press.

Redding, S. (2000). *Parents and learning.* Geneva, Switzerland: UNESCO Publications. Retrieved from http://www.ibe.unesco.org/publications /EducationalPracticesSeriesPdf/prac02e.pdf

Ronsini, V. (2009). Television representations and symbolic reproduction of inequality. *International Journal of Communication, 3,* 683–694.

Shohamy, E. (2006). *Language policy: Hidden agendas and new approaches.* New York, NY: Routledge.

Van Voorhis, F. L. (2011). Adding families to the homework equation: A longitudinal study of mathematical achievement. *Education and Urban Society, 43*(3), 313–338.

Vatterott, C. (2009). *Rethinking homework: Best practices that support diverse needs.* Alexandria, VA: Association for Supervision and Curriculum Development.

Warren, M. R., & Mapp, K. L. (2011). *A match on dry grass: Community organizing as a catalyst for school reform.* Oxford, UK: Oxford University Press.

CHAPTER 4

Broadening Conceptions of Community in Engagement

This, then, is the great humanistic and historical task of the oppressed: to liberate themselves and their oppressors as well.

—Paulo Freire (2003, p. 21)

Key Concepts: engagement triad, path of least resistance, collectivism, individualism, savior complex

INTRODUCTION

The aim of this chapter is to examine the broken engagement triad—home, school, and community. We problematize fixed notions of key stakeholders in the engagement triad and the impact these notions have on preventing reciprocal relationships. We will first focus the conversation on the meaning of the word *family*. Despite the realities of today's homes, the perception of a nuclear family comprised of a mother, father, and their biological children still dominates what constitutes a family. Families who do not match this formula often find themselves in a battle to validate their worth and authenticity, which can lead to feelings of shame and inadequacy. LGBTQ couples, foster, and adoptive families, extended family members serving as primary caretakers, unwed parents, and stepparents are just a few examples of how the traditional notion of family has been challenged (Coontz, 1996; Wiesemann, 2010; Willis, 2012; Young, 1998).

Much like family, the concept of school has also been fossilized. School is recognized as a fixed location where learning occurs with teachers and administrators overseeing the process. The site itself is exclusive, with set instructions for entering and exiting, including specific hours of operation. Although such notions have been slightly modified in recent decades as alternatives to public schooling have become more popular (i.e., online learning, homeschooling), the local public school continues to remain the trusted locale for learning.

We see value in the school as a site for education and engagement, but we caution readers not to see it as a neutral space. For culturally and linguistically diverse (CLD) families as well as those who do not fit the profile of the traditional family, school buildings can feel intimidating, unwelcoming, and even stifling on entering. This is because prior experiences and interactions often frame our reality. The school building has become the respected site for learning, but if students and families don't feel welcome in this space, the hope of fostering engagement is unrealized.

The usage of the term *community* also must be examined. How does one begin to define community? Whose community? It is one of those problematic terms used to describe everything, yet it is difficult to define. Most dictionary definitions of the term *community* connect it to place, creating a very static conception. For much of the 20th century, if you asked someone to define "community," they would likely give you an answer that involved a physical location. In the 21st century, though, that primary notion of "community" has changed (Garber, 2017).

Communities in the 21st century are not only more fluid in meaning but, in many cases, they also have become something we actively choose for ourselves as a way of affirming identity and finding comradery. The focus in much of today's usage of the term *community* involves self-selection, discovery, and notions of belonging (Garber, 2017; Jepson & Clarke, 2015; Pfortmüller, 2017). Cultural associations, religious affiliations, gamers, bloggers, art enthusiasts, and sports fans are all modern examples of groups, beyond shared places of residency, to which individuals seek membership and collective ties. For many cultures, this fluid understanding of community has always been the case.

Collectivist societies tend to place conceptions of community as central to identity more so than individualist societies (Cherry, 2018; Hofstede, 1980; Hofstede & McCrae, 2004; Triandis, 1995). Rather than create distinct boundaries in how the self navigates between spaces, collectivist societies rely on the connections between those spaces and view them as foundational to the vibrancy and sustainability of life. In her summary distinguishing collectivist and individualist societies, Cherry (2018) highlights the following attributes of collectivist cultures:

- Social rules focus on promoting selflessness and putting the community needs ahead of individual needs.
- Working as a group and supporting others is essential.
- People are encouraged to do what's best for society.
- Families and communities have a central role.

Alternative terms have been used in academia to describe collectivist and individualist cultural traits and social behavior at the individual level. Markus and Kitayama (1991) substituted the words *independence* and *interdependence* to describe personal characteristics of individualism and collectivism. Triandis (1995) uses the terms *idiocentrism* and *allocentrism* to describe individualism and collectivism at the individual rather than national level. Regardless of the term used, cultural distinctions and perceptions of how community is lived out in daily contexts from culture to culture must be factored into the conversation when re-envisioning the school–family–community triad.

Questions to Consider

- To what communities do you belong?
- What meanings, if any, do they hold for you?
- Would you describe yourself as actively engaged in these communities? Why or why not?

Think about the exchange of knowledge. In many Western countries, such as the United States, questions about specific issues are often directed to trained professionals or designated institutions. If people are sick, they research which doctor has good reviews and accepts their health insurance. If people desire to buy a new car, they most likely will go to a dealership or bank to finance it. Both of these examples illustrate how a person living in an individualist society might navigate the resources of their surroundings. Yet, for many societies, this navigation process looks different because it is based on an informal network of exchanges. Who is the trusted elder or *señora* that keeps track of the happenings of the neighborhood? Who is the local *curandero(a)* that assists with illness? Which family is providing private loans to community members to buy a car if someone is unable or unwilling to work with a bank? Who in the neighborhood makes delicious cakes or tamales for order? Who takes orders for tailoring? The focus is rarely about self-gain as much as it is about figuring out who can help perform what task in order for the community to thrive. The informal networking and system of exchanges of many non-Western cultures is prevalent within many immigrant communities and CLD families attending U.S. schools. This deep-rooted informal circuit of connections and exchanges most often occurs without any knowledge of its existence by those of the dominant white culture. Consider the following scenario.

Atifa, the Community Peacekeeper

Atifa and her family came to the United States as Muslim refugees from Sudan. Upon arriving, Atifa's children began attending public school while she helped her family acclimate, find employment, and learn English. Although she maintained a local job at a nearby factory, she was known in her religious community for her art. She was a henna artist and fashionista. Families who were planning weddings or special occasions began calling her to help with their special day. She started making trips to a nearby city to buy supplies, including many of the spices and food items used to prepare specialty items for such occasions. She sold these items within her home and took orders between trips to the city for pickup and delivery. Her expertise as a henna artist, event planner, and retail supplier was common knowledge within her network.

As more Christian Sudanese relocated to the area, she noticed increasing tension between Christian and Muslim Sudanese especially at broader cultural events that involved both groups. Because both groups utilized her event-planning services and henna artistry, she became instrumental in working toward peace between the two groups. As a result, she is respected by both Christian and Muslim Sudanese and is often called on if problems arise or when incoming families arrive.

Atifa's contact information is not in the yellow pages or in an online advertisement, despite everyone within her community relying on her services and assistance. Most immigrant families know of her or quickly become connected with her because of her gifts and talents. Yet the school her children attended had no idea of her influential role in the community. After several years of the children attending the same elementary school, the staff still were unaware of the assets she brought to the community or the leadership role she offered to immigrant families enrolled at their school site.

Questions to Consider

- Why do you think educators where Atifa's children attended school had no knowledge of the role she plays in the community?
- How do we come to know about the skills and roles that families possess?
- What efforts do you make to learn about community leaders and networks within your school's families?

It is impossible to omit "locale" from the definition of community. However, as we saw with the case of Atifa, individuals can live in the same locale and never come to know the vibrant ways in which informal networks and connections are occurring, particularly if one is accustomed to and privileged by the formal systems in operation. In many ways, the concept of community can be compared to a geode or rhizome, with multiple layers happening below the surface. Much like Atifa's contributions, happenings are often unnoticed beyond the surface level.

Atifa's role within the Christian and Muslim Sudanese populations of her town is a part of her connection to her culture. As a result, the idea of self-promotion, individual acknowledgment, or even admission of her connections within her community is counter to collectivist perceptions of community. Yet, we as schools often wait for families to step up and reveal their contributions and skillsets when attempting to strengthen family engagement. Unfortunately, schools have a short list of who constitutes a parent leader based on who is currently volunteering or running for PTO/PTA positions, which often thwarts CLD community leaders from participating in existing structures. This is precisely why it is time to stop asking more of families and begin rethinking the existing structures and modes of communication that are exclusive rather than inclusive.

REVISITING *CARIÑO*

We use the concept of authentic *cariño* in several chapters of this book because it is central to our belief of what needs to occur for relationships to generate, heal, and grow. Sometimes when we engage in service-related work, a "savior complex" can occur, whereby we intentionally or unintentionally want to fix a child, family, or community (Cole, 2012). The commitment toward helping CLD families understand their new environment can often override the acknowledgment of what they bring to the relationship. As we discuss later in Chapter 6, beginning with a "pobrecito" mentality creates lasting divides that prevent healthy interactions from occurring.

The concept of authentic *cariño*, rather than love, has been identified because it entails love *and beyond*. It encompasses a deeply rooted appreciation and humility in honoring the presence of another human being, and the commitment to supporting one another so that together the "Sí, se puede" ("Yes, we can") mantra can truly unfold. If schools continue to reach out to families through news flyers, back to school nights, or longstanding school-sponsored events (e.g., "Muffins with Mommy"), the journey of Atifa's family, along with so many others, will remain unknown. Schools will continue to remain ignorant of the struggles, contributions, and successes of their narratives. As a result, parents like Atifa are unlikely to ever feel truly welcome as contributors to their children's school experiences and will continue to feel like outsiders. For critics who say, "My primary responsibility is to teach Atifa's children to my best ability before anything else," we would argue that a student's life story is the beginning of learning and serves as a frame of reference for understanding all subject matter. In order to teach, we must first come to know those we serve.

TO CULTURAL COMPETENCY AND BEYOND

Because of the work of scholars such as Gloria Ladson-Billings (1995a, 1995b) and Geneva Gay (2000, 2010), the concepts of cultural competency, culturally relevant pedagogy, and culturally responsive teaching have become common vernacular in the field of education. As a result, greater emphasis has been placed in recent decades on cultural and linguistic diversity as a focal point in educational research and pedagogical practices, with the intent of creating more equitable learning opportunities for each student. Cultural competency, in many ways, is the foundation for such initiatives. Cultural competency is the "understanding, sensitivity, and appreciation for the history, values, experiences, and lifestyles of other cultures"; it includes "having critical conversations and challenging stereotypes and prejudices" when necessary (Muñiz, 2019, p. 13). In short, it is the ability to be self-aware of one's own cultural heritage and worldview while growing in understanding and appreciation for multiple cultures and ways of doing. Those with high levels of cultural competence are able to interact and collaborate with individuals across cultures. Cultural competency is the prerequisite to culturally relevant pedagogy and culturally responsive teaching. National Education Association's *Diversity Toolkit: Cultural Competence for Educators* states: "Culturally responsive teaching is how instructional staff (and schools) demonstrate—or implement—their cultural competence" (n.d.).

Prior to current usage of the term *culturally responsive teaching*, coined by Geneva Gay in 2000, Gloria Ladson-Billings (1995a) began to build on cultural competency in education through her creation of culturally relevant pedagogy. Ladson-Billings highlights three goals for educators to achieve in the creation of more equitable learning opportunities for students:

1. Teaching must lead to academic success for all students.
2. Teaching must instill a positive sense of cultural and ethnic identities among students.
3. Teaching needs to foster students' ability to recognize and respond to social inequalities. (Ladson-Billings, 1995a, p. 160)

Gay furthers the work of Ladson-Billings by creating effective teaching strategies in which to achieve these goals. Using her own words, Gay explains culturally responsive teaching as the ability to use "the cultural knowledge, prior experiences, frames of reference, and performance styles of ethnically diverse students to make learning encounters more relevant to and effective for them" (Gay, 2000, p. 29). Like Ladson-Billings, Gay emphasizes the importance of communicating high expectations, developing culturally relevant curriculum, offering asset-based, student-centered instruction, and fostering critical reflection.

Since the 2000s, teacher education programs across the nation have utilized the works of Ladson-Billings and Gay in preparing teachers for the demographics of today's classrooms. Despite this progress, educators attempting to build culturally responsive spaces often emphasize the representation of cultures within classrooms rather than detecting and responding to individual and systematic biases. New America, a centrist think tank on education and social policy, devised a widely utilized set of competencies for working toward culturally responsive teaching (CRT) (see Figure 4.1).

Figure 4.1. Eight Competencies for Culturally Responsive Teaching

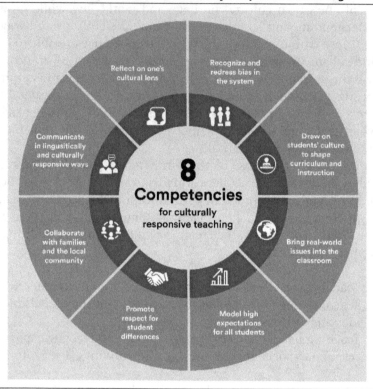

Source: Muñiz, 2019, Figure 1, p. 12, reprinted in original form under the Creative Commons Attribution 4.0 International license available at files.eric.ed.gov/fulltext /ED594599.pdf

Muñiz (2019) recently completed an in-depth national study to examine the degree to which each state embeds these competencies in teacher certification requirements. The report acknowledges that every state incorporates elements of culturally responsive practices to some degree, but argues that most requirements are minimal. States often set broad goals but provide little support on how schools should accomplish them. The report ranks the breadth and depth of each of the eight competencies for CRT across states, emphasizing that only 3 of the 50 states (i.e., Alabama, Minnesota, and Washington) include a reflective piece in their standards requiring educators to look at their own cultural lens and biases (Muñiz, 2019).

Guiding competencies and principles are solid first steps to initiate conversations on how to improve practice. However, in our experiences in the field, educators tend to prioritize certain competencies over others. Finding ways to incorporate students' cultures within a lesson or at a school function seems more manageable and less "political" than tackling systematic bias. This likely is why only three of the states mentioned above focus on this particular competency. If not careful, cultural competency can quickly become an educational buzzword that replaces the multiculturalism craze that occurred at the end of the 20th century. Although early notions of multicultural education were essential for introducing discussion of cultural diversity, they were apolitical and lacked a critical component.

Two of multiculturalism's foundational tenets included creating inclusive spaces and promoting cultural diversity. These tenets still serve as the primary focus when attempting to interact with CLD families. Yet, as evident in many attempts to build cultural competency today, they are still concepts led by white mainstream society that imply, "come and join us." No amount of international dinners or cultural festivals can create the feeling of authentic *cariño* that we are advocating. To foster a sense of authentic *cariño*, there must be an examination of the usage of "us."

One of the biggest critiques of early multicultural education models, and even proponents of cultural competency, is the lack of emphasis on social justice (Nieto, 2002; Sleeter, 2014; Sleeter & McLaren, 1995). Critical pedagogist Sonia Nieto (2002) challenges educators to ask difficult questions of ourselves and of our system, such as, "'Who's taking calculus?' 'Which classes meet in the basement?' or 'Who's teaching the children?'" (Nieto, 2002, pp. 8–9). Multicultural initiatives, according to Nieto, can quickly become an "assimilationist agenda," if not rooted in critical reflection and a commitment to antibias policies and practices (Nieto, 1995).

There are great inequalities in U.S. society and its educational system. Schools show a tremendous lack of awareness, care, and understanding when they expect CLD families to share in the culture of the school community, without the school community first standing together to name and address inequalities that occur daily. Poverty, unequal resources between school districts, hate crimes occurring in communities, and job and housing discrimination are real issues. As Justice Sonia Sotomayor once said, "None of us can afford to be bystanders in life" (speech quoted in Golden-Vazquez, 2017). Therefore, how do we begin to acknowledge the bias in our communities, schools, and even within ourselves?

Advocating for our families is about more than having a translator present at a potluck. It is about examining how daily practices are reinforcing alienating spaces and inequalities and then working together to change them. Part of this process requires educators to acknowledge how current spaces and systems are benefiting the dominant group. In order to begin such reflection, a *critical consciousness* is required. Brazilian educator and social theorist Paulo Freire coined the term *critical consciousness*, which begins with an examination of the status quo (Freire, 1970). Specifically, critical conscientization is the process of recognizing oppressive systems in the world and how one's positionality impacts and/or contributes to their perpetuation. It allows a person to recognize social and political contradictions and call for social action as part of this new understanding or consciousness (Mustakova-Possardt, 2003). Educators who advocate for a critical consciousness are often labeled as "radical," "leftist," or even "socialist." Yet, fostering authentic *cariño* is reliant on our feeling deeply for one another, humbly unlearning divisive ways of thinking and doing, and envisioning a tomorrow that reflects the voices of all community members.

To lay a foundation for authentic *cariño*, educators need to learn about the families they serve as well as their respective cultures and values. Moreover, educators must find ways to make connections as supporters and members of their school's surrounding geographical community. Sometimes, it feels more natural to compartmentalize aspects of our daily lives, especially when living in an individualistic culture. As a result, educators (particularly white educators in schools with high CLD populations) often live in communities outside the neighborhoods they teach, frequent restaurants and places of business beyond the boundary of their school or district, and rely solely on interactions within the walls of the school to build relationships (Emdin, 2016).

Taking It to the Streets

Traditional interactions that occur at the school site or through take-home surveys and questionnaires tend to elicit limited responses when it comes to re-envisioning the triad. Part of the problem beyond not spending quality time together is not knowing what to ask when you have the opportunity. There are multiple ways of gathering information about the assets of a school–family–community triad. Nevertheless, it cannot happen without attempting to reach out to families outside the school's walls and learning to listen. This begins with strengthening one's commitment to understanding cultural differences and recognizing biases. It can further grow through establishing ties and learning about families by getting into the community.

As educators, we can broaden the local barbershops, laundromats, bakeries, restaurants and parks we frequent thereby increasing our chances of encountering and greeting families. Where are people walking? Are there street vendors? Where are kids playing? Schools that decide to "take it to the streets" can consider a schoolwide canvassing initiative designed to have educators interact with community members with the intention to learn. Specifically, ask families and community members what suggestions they have for improving their school, and how the school can better support their needs. Look for common themes to help frame dialogues. Ask about the neighborhood and its members as well as its history, even if the history is divisive. We have encountered multiple examples of teachers not knowing instances of racial segregation that occurred within their school's town. As a result, teachers were ignorant of some of the deep-rooted hurt or cultural conflicts hindering family and community engagement. Such initiatives are most effective, however, when teachers remain humble and demonstrate *cariño*. Again, see this as a *listening* tour. This approach to relationship building may feel very uncomfortable for educators who are used to providing the information, or receiving information within the bounds of their own terms.

It is naïve to think that sending a bunch of teachers out as part of an in-service would strengthen relationships. The last thing many families want is to be interviewed; however, they *do want* to feel listened to and validated. There is a difference. That is why we suggest not going out with a particular agenda but rather approaching the outing as an opportunity to interact and seek understanding. Public health advocates and street educators have gone into neighborhoods for decades to reach out and inform the public about particular issues. Although we use this example to show precedence, our suggestion is not to educate or inform. Rather, it is quite the opposite. We feel it is important for educators to learn from the community-at-large. Regular visits to the community are needed for families to establish trust and seek understanding. We stress the word *regular* because going into the community must become an ongoing and organic part of a school's commitment to strengthening family and community engagement. We as educators can't criticize families for low attendance and school functions when we aren't seen regularly within the neighborhoods, organizations, and businesses of families whose children we teach.

Home visits are another approach to learning about the happenings within a school's population. However, like many school-sponsored events, home visits are often formulated interactions that are "conducted" based on a set agenda, with the teacher doing most of the talking. Much like neighborhood canvassing, culturally responsive practices should be a prerequisite to any teacher conducting a home visit. Ernst-Slavit and Mason (n.d.) provide helpful tips when rethinking home visits to reflect collaboration and relational trust rather than school-centric agendas that invite cultural mishaps. Countless bits of information can be learned by talking less and listening more to those in one's surroundings.

Now What?

After undertaking multiple outings beyond the walls of the school to actively learn and listen as educators, the next question becomes, "What's next?" The answer: "Keep doing it!" Trust takes time.

Schools also can work to create an asset-based community inventory. Build a team at your school site willing to develop a contact list for your school's community. During the political times in which we live, inventories and lists can feel invasive and even threatening. We are not suggesting disclosing personal information about families and students. Individual files and student records shared between teachers are completely different than a community-based assets inventory. In Chapter 3, we introduced the concept of *manualidades* when rethinking homework. What are the skills of your school's families? How can schools see the assets of each family? Who sells Halal products? Which families run hair salons that specialize in black hair products? Is there a family who sells *pupusas* (thick flat bread) from their home? Perhaps there is a local food truck that schools can contact to order food for in-services, rather than using a franchise like Panera's, Dominos, or Subway? Remember, the term *asset* is synonymous with *gifts* and *talents*, and our community's assets should always be treated as such.

TRADITIONAL PARTNERS WITH A TWIST

When analyzing the concept of community, it is important to rethink the meaning of community partners. Who are the current partners of your school? Community partners are often described as organizations and businesses interested in collaborating in the happenings of the school and its greater surroundings. Sometimes formal partnerships with local businesses form in order to receive funding for school programs. Discount cards sold by sports teams are a common way schools reach out to involve businesses. Donations for technology, field maintenance, or building renovations are other ways local businesses and organizations invest financially as community partners. Similar to the recommendation for school–family dynamics, the rapport between schools and local businesses/organizations needs to be rooted in respect, collaboration, and reciprocity. Too often, local businesses and organizations are notified of upcoming events or contacted when supplies are needed for such events. Instead, what would happen if community partners were asked to brainstorm about issues pertaining to the school? There have been several examples of creative ideas that have come together by listening to families and community partners.

One example that has received media attention in recent years has been the partnering of school librarians and laundromats. Families often spend enormous amounts of time at laundromats with little stimulation for the children (Humphries, 2019; Williams, 2018). Several communities have brainstormed with laundromats in their areas to create spaces where reading corners are established, and each Saturday librarians go and read stories to the children. Such an initiative has positive implications for families, teachers, business owners, and students. It takes creative thinking and collaboration to foster reciprocal partnerships.

Another example that has taken off in recent years is the Whirlpool Care Counts program. Teachers and administrators across the country have shared stories about students and the connection between absenteeism and the availability of hygiene products and laundry services. Thanks to programs such as the Whirlpool Care Counts program, numerous schools have established free laundry facilities before and after school hours for families to utilize. These moments when families are accessing laundry services are opportunities for strengthening relations. If carefully planned, schools can destigmatize and normalize the process of using the laundry facilities, to avoid families feeling embarrassed. For example, staff can be encouraged to utilize the facility before and after school. While clothes are washing, families can be invited to assist students getting off the bus in the morning or to read stories to children in after-school programs. As shared by a K–8 principal in Fairfield, California, whose school benefited from the Whirlpool program, "It's easy to be judgmental of parents whose children don't come to school if you don't have a frame of reference for their situations . . ." (Tate, 2016). The laundry program is a perfect example of how needs were identified and collaboration extended beyond the school with business partners wanting to give.

Once needs are identified authentically, community partners are almost always willing to help. The problem for sponsors and partners is that there is often little clarity in how to collaborate. Much like school communication with families, there generally is a unidirectional conversation, in which educators are the communicators who ask for something from community partners. As a result, community partners continue to assist with funding renovations on sports fields, donating supplies, or enhancing technology in the schools without a relational investment that is lasting and impactful.

Similar to families we serve, community partners do not fit a particular mold, yet the idea of community partners has become fossilized in the mindset of schools. Schools tend to see partners as restaurants, grocery stores, or even nonprofit foundations who donate funding. However, going back to geodes and rhizomes, what are some of the less familiar businesses, clubs, and organizations that may want to connect with the local school? Some of these organizations may have little to no money, or may be loosely formed as an affiliate. However, they may possess great influence with school families. As educators, we need to rethink the meaning of assets when approaching partnerships.

It's Time to Lose Control

With any profession, there are cultural norms and ways of doing things. At times, we take comfort in the roles we play and even absolve ourselves of responsibility and accountability for making change. After all, it is easier to say, "That is how it has always been done." Sociologist Alan Johnson (2014) examines this mindset within social systems, such as schools, and refers to it as "the path of least resistance" (p. 19). We sometimes go along with a set of policies because we run into less resistance than if we do otherwise. This is particularly true for young professionals who, for good reason, are worried about maintaining their positions instead of working toward viable change. As faculty mentors, we have witnessed firsthand young teachers who are fearful of trying new ideas due to pressures linked to test preparation. Administrators can also portray this worry and feel they must prioritize practicalities over possibilities due to the social hierarchy embedded in the organizational structure of schools. As a result, family engagement is often linked exclusively to students' academic performance, or it remains only a secondary priority.

A core question to ask is: Who is driving? What might a school look like if families had the chance to drive? This does not mean giving more responsibilities or roles to parents, such as sitting on advisory boards, serving as homeroom parents, or attending more PTO/PTA meetings (with the same dedicated families selling brownies or collecting box tops). Instead, what if families were able to set the parameters that helped foster relations within the engagement triad? This dynamic would require more servant leadership practices on the part of administrators and educators as well as the support and understanding of grassroots initiatives.

In their text, *A Match on Dry Grass*, Warren and Mapp (2011) analyze grassroots initiatives in six different communities predominantly comprised of CLD families in urban regions across the United States. They explore how to shift effective community change from being a top-down process to a bottom-up process, arguing that the best agents of change in establishing strong relations are the students, families, and community residents. In many of these examples, neighborhoods met regularly to discuss desires for their children and needs they wanted addressed in order to improve partnerships with schools. Yet, before initiatives began and change occurred, these groups first focused on nourishing their "roots," or family assets and traditions that brought them together in support of their children and community. Using a tree metaphor illustrated in Figure 4.2, Warren and Mapp examine transformational change that has occurred by such initiatives. Traditions for how and where organizing occurs can vary greatly, from parks to churches to hair salons to schools. The key is recognizing and honoring relationships built on the stories of families and relational trust.

School leaders tend to homogenize parental engagement, even when it is framed as initiatives designed to embrace diversity. This occurs when we reduce the influence of cultural diversity of CLD families to events highlighting the food, clothing, games, and cultural traditions of each group. However, ways of seeing, communicating, and interacting with one another also vary and are affected by cultural, linguistic, and economic differences. The authentic emergence of engagement and the growing cultivation and reliance on relationships are more important than any planned event.

Figure 4.2. Community Capacity Approach: A Relational Approach to Authentic Partnerships

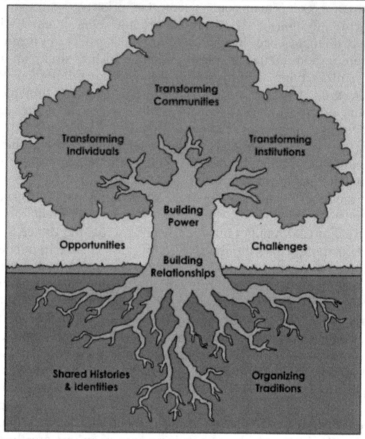

Source: Warren & Mapp, 2011, Figure 1.1, p. 15

Family organizing initiatives, such as the examples discussed in Warren and Mapp's (2011) text, can be found across the country. They help parents navigate school politics and find creative ways to work toward change. Yet, for many school administrators, these types of initiatives can feel intimidating and even threatening. As school officials, we are used to being at the table making decisions and determining how to address issues as they arise. Meetings outside of the school, where families discuss school politics and procedures without the presence of school officials, are distinct from traditional practices of local schools. In such cases, school officials tend to personalize such efforts and even interpret them as adversarial, especially if families are feeling frustrated or marginalized. After all (according to mainstream thinking), the role of teachers and administrators is to "lead" the school community.

School officials are accustomed to interacting directly with parents through groups such as the PTO/PTA. Yet look at which families are attending these meetings? Are your CLD families actively involved? Is the school directly monitoring the agenda and priorities of such groups? It is a natural inclination to fear and even judge what we don't understand. For marginalized parents, a way back to the conversation with schools is often finding a safe space to work through the frustration, confusion, intimidation, and possibly hurt that has occurred through relations with schools. Such spaces and opportunities for healing commonly occur outside the walls of the school. How can we as educators support grassroots parent groups? If such groups currently do not exist, how might they? Leadership must shift from *leading* to *supporting* when growing family engagement. As knowledge of such grassroots efforts reaches the school, administrators can celebrate them, offer support, and wait for the families to come forward with ideas. Then, we all need to be ready to listen.

Questions to Consider

- What are the needs of your community?
- How did you come to know of these needs?
- How are they currently being addressed?
- Who is leading the conversation?
- What is the end goal?

Well-Intentioned Efforts That Have Yielded Limited Results

As discussed in previous chapters, the concept of family engagement has been a growing priority for schools not only because of federal policy mandates but also due to research that links academic achievement with parental involvement (Bus, van Ijzendoorn, & Pellegrini, 1995; Jeynes, 2003; Wilder, 2014). As a result, numerous resources exist on ways schools can engage their families. Approaches have varied in scope, size, and frequency. Through our work, we have noticed that schools are beginning to go beyond their walls to enhance family and community engagement. Literacy nights held in apartment complex multipurpose rooms, back-to-school ice cream socials at local parks, and teacher visits to student homes in lieu of parent–teacher conferences are just a few examples of how educators are attempting to step outside the school locale to engage families.

Our intention is not to define the ideal event that will maximize family and community engagement nor to reinvent a definition for engagement. Rather, it is to examine the word *engagement* itself and begin to rewind. The tendency of educators and most service providers when organizing events is to set an objective, make plans, implement, and assess outcomes. In fact, this is the basis of all educational training. This process may or may not be collaborative, but the emphasis is most always on the event or plan being implemented. The success of such events is largely determined by foot traffic. How many attended? Schools commonly must report attendance at community and family engagement events for grant purposes and funding reports. These events, no matter how well executed, how many people attended, or where they occurred (on- or off-site), simply reflect points in time. The focus is always the event and, like all events, they come and go. A committee may debrief the highs and lows, but the focus quickly shifts to the next event. In other words, even if families and community partners participated in the planning process of an event, the event itself is usually still school-centric; it is driven by the goals of the school staff in an attempt to foster relations.

CONCLUSION

It is time to rethink the triad. The first step is to change its shape. Triads are hierarchical and reliant on corners that limit the interaction between participants. In our re-envisioning of school–family–community partnerships, we prefer the usage of a circle as the visual image, because it supports continual movement, inclusion, and flow.

Families with caregivers who do not respond to the names "mom and dad" look different and are different. Additionally, schools are not the only locale where families and educators can interact; as such, they should not be the sole focus of learning. If we limit our conceptions of family and community, and we limit our interactions and learning to the confines of schools, then possibilities for engagement are limited as well. A community is constantly evolving and must encompass those who see themselves as a part of it, rather than circumscribe membership and belonging to its geographical position. Families, students, local businesses, organizations, clubs, and educators all need to feel recognized.

We encourage readers to create a school community that is constantly in motion, reliant on trust derived from listening and fostering authentic, humble, and respectful relations. Everything else will follow.

Check It Out
(Questions to Guide Reflection and Discussion)

---

1. Critically reflect on the ways your school site has approached family engagement:
   • Make a list of all the ways that your school site is currently attempting to reach out to families.
   • Place an asterisk next to the examples listed that you think are effective. Why do you think these attempts are effective? How do they differ from the examples that are not effective?

Plan It Out
(Creating an Idea That Requires Action)

---

2. In a team, think and act on the following:
   • What steps need to occur to support a systemic paradigm shift from merely *recognizing roles* in the triad to *fostering relationships*?
   • What might a community assets plan look like for your school?
   • Is there a way to invite families to share community resources and entrepreneurial endeavors (e.g., community centers, multiethnic stores, services) with incoming families?
   • How can your school team begin entering into the community with *cariño*?

Try It Out
(Attempting Action and Reflecting upon Outcomes)

---

3. In tandem with enacting at least one of your planned actions, determine:
   • How will you measure the success of the new action?
   • What nontraditional measures will you create and/or propose for receiving feedback from CLD families?

Momentos de Reflexión (Moments of Reflection)

1. In what ways can I better demonstrate authentic *cariño* in my classroom?
2. How will I strengthen and act on my commitment to understanding cultural differences and recognizing biases?
3. How will I listen to and validate the students and families of our school community in meaningful ways? How will I encourage colleagues to do the same?

REFERENCES

Bus, A., Van Ijzendoorn, M., & Pellegrini, A. (1995). Joint book reading makes for success in learning to read: A meta-analysis on intergenerational transmission of literacy. *Review of Educational Research, 65*(1), 1–21.

Cherry, K. (2018). *Understanding collectivist cultures: How culture can influence behavior.* Retrieved from www.verywellmind.com/what-are-collectivistic-cultures-2794962

Cole, T. (2012, March 21). *The white-savior industrial complex.* Retrieved from www.theatlantic.com/international/archive/2012/03/the-white-savior-industrialcomplex/254843

Coontz, S. (1996). The way we weren't: Myth and reality of the 'traditional' family. *The National Forum, 76*(4), 45–48.

Emdin, C. (2016). *For white folks who teach in the hood.* Boston, MA: Beacon Press.

Ernst-Slavit, G., & Mason, M. (n.d.). *Making your first ELL home visit: A guide for classroom teachers.* Retrieved from www.colorincolorado.org/article/making-your-first-ell-home-visit-guide-classroom-teachers

Freire, P. (1970). *Pedagogy of the oppressed.* New York, NY: Continuum.

Freire, P. (2003). *Pedagogy of the oppressed* (30th anniversary ed.). New York, NY: Continuum.

Garber, M. (2017, July 3). *What does "community" mean? The term's evolution makes a nice metaphor for the rise of American individualism—and the decline of trust in American institutions.* Retrieved from www.theatlantic.com/entertainment/archive/2017/07/what-does-community-mean/532518

Gay, G. (2000). *Culturally responsive teaching: Theory, research, and practice.* New York, NY: Teachers College Press.

Gay, G. (2010). *Culturally responsive teaching: Theory, research, and practice* (2nd ed.). New York, NY: Teachers College Press.

Golden-Vazquez, A. (2017, April 3). *Justice Sonia Sotomayor speaks out on Latino identity and civic engagement.* Retrieved from www.aspeninstitute.org/blog-posts/justice-sonia-sotomayor-speaks-latino-identity-civic-engagement

Hofstede, G. (1980). *Culture's consequences: International differences in work-related values.* Beverly Hills, CA: Sage.

Hofstede, G., & McCrae, R. R. (2004). Culture and personality revisited: Linking traits and dimensions of culture. *Cross-Cultural Research, 38*(1), 52–88.

Humphries, M. (2019, June 12). *Kids are learning to read in a place you'd never expect: The laundromat.* Retrieved from nationswell.com/laundromat-literacy-programs

Jepson, A., & Clarke, A. (Eds.). (2015). *Exploring community festivals and events.* Abingdon, UK: Routledge.

Jeynes, W. H. (2003). A meta-analysis: The effects of parental involvement on minority children's academic achievement. *Education & Urban Society, 35*(2), 202–218.

Johnson, A. (2014). *The forest and the trees: Sociology as life, practice, and promise* (3rd ed.). Philadelphia, PA: Temple University Press.

Ladson-Billings, G. (1995a). But that's just good teaching! The case for culturally relevant pedagogy. *Theory into Practice, 34*(3), 159–165.

Ladson-Billings, G. (1995b). Toward a theory of culturally relevant pedagogy. *American Educational Research Journal, 32*(3), 465–491.

Markus, H. R., & Kitayama, S. (1991). Culture and the self: Implications for cognition, emotion, and motivation. *Psychological Review, 20,* 568–579.

Muñiz, J. (2019). *Culturally responsive teaching: A 50-state survey on teaching standards.* New America. Retrieved from files.eric.ed.gov/fulltext/ED594599.pdf

Mustakova-Possardt, E. (2003). *Critical consciousness: A study of morality in global, historical context.* London, UK: Praeger.

National Education Association. (n.d.). *Diversity toolkit: Cultural competence for educators.* Retrieved from www.nea.org/tools/30402.htm

Nieto, S. (1995). From brown heroes and holidays to assimilationist agendas: Reconsidering the critiques of multicultural education. In C. E. Sleeter & P. L. McLaren (Eds.), *Multicultural education, critical pedagogy, and the politics of difference* (pp. 191–220). Albany: State University of New York Press.

Nieto, S. (2002). Profoundly multicultural questions. *Educational Leadership, 60*(4), 6–10.

Pfortmüller, F. (2017). *What does "community" even mean? A definition attempt & conversation starter.* Retrieved from medium.com/@pforti/what-does-community-even-mean-a-definition-attempt-conversation-starter-9b443fc523d0

Sleeter, C. (2014). Multiculturalism and education for citizenship in the context of neoliberalism. *Intercultural Education, 25*(2), 85–94.

Sleeter, C., & McLaren, P. (Eds.). (1995). *Multicultural education and critical pedagogy: The politics of difference.* New York: State University of New York Press.

Tate, A. S. (2016). *Schools find one simple answer to attendance problem: Washing machines.* Retrieved from www.today.com/parents/schools-find-one-simple-answer-attendance-problem-washing-machines-t101318

Triandis, H. (1995). *Individualism and collectivism.* New York, NY: Westview Press.

Warren, M. R., & Mapp, K. L. (2011). *A match on dry grass: Community organizing as a catalyst for school reform.* New York, NY: Oxford University Press.

Wiesemann, C. (2010). The moral challenge of natality: Towards a post-traditional concept of family and privacy in repro-genetics. *New Genetics and Society, 29*(1), 61–71.

Wilder, S. (2014). Effects of parental involvement on academic achievement: A meta-synthesis. *Educational Review, 66*(3), 377–397.

Williams, J. (2018). Literacy at the laundromat. *U.S. News and World Report.* Retrieved from www.usnews.com/news/healthiest-communities/articles/2018-12-25/library-laundromat-program-puts-spin-on-child-literacy

Willis, M. (2012). Insights: The myth of the traditional family. *Parenting for High Potential, 1*(5), 14, 16.

Young, A. (1998). Reconceiving the family: Challenging the paradigm of the exclusive family. *American University Journal of Gender and the Law, 6*(3), 505–556.

CHAPTER 5

Planting on Fertile Ground

ESL/Dual Language Programs
and Parental Engagement

My culture values the sacredness of *el maíz* (corn). I have memories that
fill my mind of my making tortillas and tamales with my family, and seeing the countryside of my homeland.

—Señora Isabel (DLBE program parent, personal communication, 2017)

> **Key Concepts:** dynamic bilingualism, boutique mentality, language
> commodification, radical kinship

INTRODUCTION

Nationwide, our PK–12 schools serve approximately 4.5 million English learners (ELs) (also known as emergent bilinguals) (NCES,
2016). ELs represent an array of cultures and languages, and their
presence in our classroom has the potential to make our instruction more meaningful and fruitful. However, research suggests that
teachers serving ELs often feel ill-equipped to support the academic,
linguistic, cultural, and cognitive needs of their students (de Jong &
Harper, 2005). Within the context of English as a second language
(ESL) or English for students of other languages (ESOL) classrooms,
family engagement requires teachers to shift their perspectives.

In ESL/ESOL classrooms, students are provided with scaffolds to
acquire the target language. Students frequently are placed in ESOL
classes with other ELs with either similar or different language proficiency levels in order to receive "sheltered instruction." That is, they
receive academic content modification that integrates language and

content instruction using grade-level–appropriate materials and comprehensible input. In some cases, ELs are pulled out of their classes to receive ESL services, or teachers are able to offer "push in" ESL services during instruction. The ESL/ESOL program adopted depends on the school district/division's approach to ESL/ESOL instruction, allocation of funds, and professional resources. Still, by law (see *Castañeda v. Pickard*, 1978; Every Student Succeeds Act [ESSA], 2015; *Lau v. Nichols*, 1974), ELs are entitled to receive equal and equitable education in our classrooms.

One option for providing equitable education for ELs is the implementation of bilingual education programs, particularly dual language bilingual education (DLBE) programs, also known as two-way bilingual education (TWBE) programs. The overarching goals featured in these programs are biliteracy, bilingualism, and cross-cultural communication (Christian, 2006). DLBE programs have been implemented using different models; they may use a 50/50 model or a 90/10, with ratios referring to the language of instruction used to teach content-area subjects. In a 50/50 model, students are taught in English 50% of the instructional time and in the partnering language the other 50% (Thomas & Collier, 2012). Likewise, in a 90/10 model, students are taught in the partnering language 90% of the time and in English the other 10%. In this particular model, the language distribution changes as students move on toward higher grade levels, with an increasing proportion of English being used. Student demographics also play a significant role in implementing a DLBE program. Ideally, the student demographic composition in the classroom will feature 50% of native English speakers and 50% of native speakers in the partnering language.

Over the years, various theories and models on bilingual education have emerged. Many of these programs, however, have been criticized for promoting subtractive bilingualism. Programs such as transitional bilingual education, integrated bilingual education, and developmental bilingual education use students' native language as a conduit to learn the target language (i.e., English). Once the learner has acquired the target language, instruction in the first language is discontinued. By contrast, programs such as heritage language programs, DLBE, and one-way immersion programs are tasked with promoting and fostering development in the first language and second language so that students become bilingual/multilingual individuals. Such programs foster additive bilingualism practices by supporting the importance of learning both languages while honoring the identities of the students

(Cummins, 1979). García (2009) offers a different perspective on bilingualism. She uses the term *dynamic bilingualism,* which highlights the gamma of students' linguistic repertoires and how they act in conjunction to become one language unit.

Questions to Consider

- Do you feel your school site utilizes subtractive, additive, or dynamic approaches to language learning?
- How is multilingualism an asset in the classroom?

LEVELING THE GROUND: ADDRESSING CHALLENGES OF ESL AND DLBE SETTINGS FOR CLD FAMILIES

As discussed throughout this book, culturally and linguistically diverse (CLD) families are often marginalized from the daily happenings within public schools due to language constraints, schedule conflicts often tied to shift work, cultural misunderstandings on school procedures and expectations, or simply feeling uncomfortable or unwelcome. In ESL programs, the challenge is compounded by the lack of preparation and support preservice and in-service teachers are offered throughout their careers to respond to the assets and needs of CLD students. Such a scenario makes it difficult for teachers to negotiate opportunities to interact with and learn from CLD communities. Teachers often ask, "How do I reach out to families if I am unfamiliar with the language and/or culture?" When approaching the answer to this question, we gently encourage teachers to transform their anxieties into an action stance and begin with gathering information:

- How many languages and cultures are represented in my classroom?
- What are the biographies of my students?
- Is my classroom library congruent with my students' languages and cultures?
- What school/division resources do I have available so that I can connect with families in meaningful ways?

As explored in Chapter 2, when language use is not negotiated in effective ways, it has the potential to hinder the involvement of CLD families. Therefore, conducting language inventories at the school level to identify which languages are represented in the student population, as well as finding key individuals at the community level who can act as linguistic resources or bridges, becomes crucial to developing spaces where CLD families feel comfortable and welcome. School administrators and teachers must begin this process by creating a physical environment that represents the culture and languages of their families while recruiting staff equipped to answer questions and mediate cultural, linguistic, and logistic needs. In the sections that follow in this chapter, we take a closer look at the challenges as well as possibilities of ESL and DLBE programs in the creation of more inclusive spaces.

Challenges of Dual Language Bilingual Education Programs

The intention of DLBE programs is to begin with a cohort of families that represent the English language and the partnering language (e.g., Spanish, French, Chinese) who will continue throughout the program. Most often, the program exists at the elementary level but can often continue through middle school and high school in some form, depending on the school district. Because the population of the DLBE program at a given school is a microcosm of the school's larger population, lack of connection between CLD families and native English-speaking families can be more obvious.

In addition to the size of the program being much smaller than the general school population, DLBE programs are typically comprised of only two language groups. In larger school populations and even ESL programs, multiple languages and cultures are present. In DLBE programs, even though multiple cultures may be represented in the program's population (i.e., racial and ethnic diversity among native English speakers or diverse cultural representations among native Spanish speakers with families from various countries in a Spanish/English program), there still exists an obvious linguistic line between parents who speak English and the partnering language. Families representing both language communities want their children to experience the linguistic and cultural benefits of DLBE programs but often have very few tools to interact with each other. As a result, distinct groups often formulate at school events between the two sets of families, those who speak English and those who do not. And, since the majority of English-speaking participants within DLBE programs tend to be white and middle class (Morales & Maravilla, 2019; Williams, 2017), racial and socioeconomic lines can further solidify these groups.

Flores and García (2017) wrote a compelling article describing current-day DLBE programs as "boutique" programs. Our experiences working with DLBE programs across the country supports this critique. Enrollment in DLBE programs has become very competitive. Because DLBE programs are used by schools to deliver language instruction and strengthen language comprehension for EL learners, filling the available spaces for native speakers of the partnering language is often a relatively fluid process based on school personnel decisions, with the approval of families. As a result, lengthy applications and lotteries are most generally designed for the numerous native English speakers wanting to join. Long waiting lists are common, filled with white families pushing to get their children in so that they become bilingual. This can sometimes become quite political not only between families wanting a space in the program but also within the school community at large. Administrators have talked about the struggle of balancing the focus, excitement, and enrollment frenzy of DLBE programs amid families not enrolled and teachers not a part of the program. Part of this balancing act requires administrators to proactively situate DLBE as one of many ways their school honors language and cultural diversity, with examples to share of additional happenings within the school. Otherwise, conflict and dissent can occur as families and staff begin to see the DLBE program as the "favorite" of the school, receiving extra attention, more exciting instruction, and sometimes special funding.

Referencing back to the analogy of a boutique, customers who shop at such locations often feel a sense of entitlement and come to expect a certain level of customer service as a result. Flores and García (2017) reflect on such feelings of entitlement by white families who expect not only a place in the DLBE programs but also special attention upon entering. Consequently, DLBE teachers can find their time dominated by eager native English-speaking families who want to know all the details about DLBE instruction, how to assist their children in learning the partnering language, lessening anxiety if reading levels in English appear lower at the onset, and so forth. Unfortunately, CLD families representing the partnering language do not always receive the same level of attention as the native English speakers, due to time constraints or an absence of the cultural capital shared between teachers and native English families. This phenomenon can be transferred to students, as well.

When examining the different student populations within DLBE, concerns exist regarding perceptions of program benefits for different subgroups (Cervantes-Soon, 2014; Izquierdo, 2011; Porter, 2018). DLBE is often viewed as a necessity for struggling ELs to gain basic English competency. For native English-speaking students, it is described as an opportunity for upward mobility linked to perceptions of giftedness. We must consider: How are these differing perceptions manifested in the interpersonal relations between peers of each language group? Educators and students? Educators and families? Families from each language group?

Due to a shortage of teachers who are native speakers of the partnering language, many of the teachers across the country teaching in DLBE programs are doing so as second language learners themselves. As a result, English becomes the default language spoken at school functions, which serves to reinforce cultural commonalities between DLBE educators and native English speakers. The ramifications can have negative consequences for CLD families, leading them to feel unwelcome and less likely to engage with the DLBE program or larger school.

Cultural divisions between native English-speaking and CLD families, the unequal balance of time given to CLD families based on expectations and shared cultural capital, and the overuse of English as the medium for communication all contribute to the greatest challenge of DLBE programs: *language commodification*. Language commodification, a term used within linguistic anthropology, is the process of reducing language to a commodity or an economic resource (Heller, 2010). One of the main tenets of DLBE programs is to enhance cultural competency and intercultural understanding. Yet, driven by the demands of white English-speaking families and coupled by school districts in search of an instructional model to assist with growing EL populations, the focus of DLBE programs has been reduced to language acquisition. CLD families within DLBE programs might be invited to speak on their cultural traditions or participate in an annual potluck, but the cultural history and integrity that comprises the partnering language is often absent in classroom instruction as well as interactions between families and school personnel.

Question to Consider

- As teachers, how can we ensure ESL and DLBE programs are designed and implemented using a lens of inclusion and equity?

Aside from introductory classroom activities focusing on family histories or geographical icons (i.e., flags and maps) of represented countries, DLBE programs largely have not been able to cultivate cultural connections that lead to a deeper respect and understanding of difference. For native English speakers, this results in learning a new language without gaining cultural context or developing a respect for cultural diversity. For ELs, this lack of emphasis on cultural histories results in a "sanitizing" or "whitewashing" effect, turning language into a commodity for an already empowered group (Cervantes-Soon, 2014; Izquierdo, 2011; Valdés, 1997). For both groups, there is a missed opportunity to begin fostering relationships. Take a moment to reflect on the following vignette.

La Señora Lupe y Sus Tamales Sagrados (Mrs. Lupe and Her Sacred Tamales)

Like many immigrants who come to the United States in search of economic stability for their families, Lupe came to the United States from Mexico when she was 17 years old. She left her son to be raised by her mother. She had grown up living in an extremely small village in the state of Oaxaca. Her father had died when she was a child. Lupe, her younger brother, Carlos, and their mother comprised their family. They survived on their family's small farm. Yet Oaxaca was experiencing significant drought, which put her family in economic desperation. The decision was made that Carlos would stay and try to salvage the farm while tending to their ailing mother and Lupe's small son. Lupe would head north to find work.

Lupe ended up in California doing domestic work before eventually making it to a hog-processing plant in North Carolina where she met her current partner, Beto. She and Beto had a son who was placed in a DLBE program upon entering kindergarten to become more English proficient. Their son is now in 4th grade. When we talked to Lupe about her recommendations for improving DLBE programs for families, she expressed the need to "see the whole person."

Lupe has been invited by her son's school to come and make tamales for the last 4 years. She talked about how she was honored to do so because she was able to share a bit of her culture with her child's class. But she admits that she feels like she is only seen as the "tamales lady" by the rest of the school. She wants to encourage children to love and honor their family's traditions, including preparing food, but is frustrated because no one from the school has ever asked her to share her story, only the steps to making tamales. "After 4 years, I am sure the kids are tired of me and making tamales."

In this instance, Lupe was never asked how she would like to contribute to her son's school. She was never consulted about the cultural traditions and biography of her family. Instead, year after year she was asked to make tamales for all to enjoy. How does this scenario exemplify the whitewashing effect described above? In this instance, the school attempted to provide cultural connections for students without inviting the family member to supply context or establishing authentic school–family–community relationships.

Prioritizing Intercultural Understanding and Radical Kinship Within DLBE Programs

As authors, we have spent a great deal of time trying to think about the best way to describe the re-envisioning of communities within DLBE programs, and schools in general. The concept that we have chosen is *radical kinship*. Kinship has been a term used in the field of anthropology and sociology for centuries (Collier & Yanagisako, 1987; Hayden, 2007; Parkin & Stone, 2004). Yet, over the years, it has been deconstructed and repurposed as communities and families continue to diversify and challenge hegemonic and heteronormative notions of human ties to one another. Once used to explain genealogical patterns connected to descent and marriage (Shenk & Mattison, 2011), new ideas of kinship began to form as early as the 1960s, influenced in part by political movements of that time, such as the civil rights movement, gay rights movement, and feminist movement that challenged existing notions of family and community (Butler, 2002; Davidoff, 2005). Today, phrases such as "voluntary kinship" and "chosen kin" have been coined to reconceptualize kinship and socioemotional ties and family bonds based on a common affinity and care for one another. Borrowing from American Jesuit priest and activist for peace and justice, Gregory Boyle, we build on the term "radical kinship" and his description of the deep and profound love required in transforming and growing relations among individuals (Boyle, 2017).

The vignette focusing on Señora Lupe provides a concrete example of how our attempts of integration and inclusion can fail if we do not understand relationships through the lens of radical kindship. In our communities as well as in our classrooms, the binary of us versus them no longer works. While Lupe was attempting to share the sacredness of *el maíz* through her cooking, she felt as though she was not afforded the opportunity to explore the fundamental meaning of the ingredients used to make *tamales* and the tenderness of her family memories while making them. Lupe is not only "the *tamales* lady"—she is an integral part of the school community as well as the classroom narrative. A perspective of radical kinship allows us to see each other as individuals and vital members of our collective narrative. Enacting radical kinship in our classrooms will help us, our students, and their families heal and flourish.

Our collective ability to thrive begins in earnest when CLD families are able to see themselves as key participants in the fabric of the school community. Their biographies and experiences are embedded in the curriculum, educational initiatives, budget meetings, library resources, and school events. Under such circumstances, feelings of fear, uncertainty, and frustration are replaced with *engagement, love,* and *collaboration.* All three constructs bolster transformative dialogue (Freire, 1970) between families and schools.

Transformative dialogue leads to a feeling of kinship, where those previously marginalized see themselves as active participants creating their narrative, and school personnel are active learners working collaboratively to change individual perceptions as well as transform the school's sociocultural context. Engaging transformative dialogue is an act of bravery reliant on the creation of deep *lazos* (ties) of kinship. Such connections allow us to find the compassion we seek in order to listen and speak with open hearts and minds. Radical kinship between families and schools may be expressed in:

- The way we interact with each other when a family walks through the door: "I am so glad to see you!"
- A holistic understanding of the construction of family (e.g., families' diverse composition, beliefs, strengths, and needs) and the multiple positionalities that exist within the school.
- Less structured meetings, where teachers and families have the time to explore the strengths of children and collaborate to identify how to better support them across both domains (home and school), rather than top-down approaches where teachers and officials "tell" families how things are going and what to do.
- Dialogue circles among families on topics chosen by parents (with language, transportation, and location carefully

negotiated in advance to enhance representation of all parents).

- Two or three family narratives featured in the school newsletter or website to highlight and value their experiences.
- Neighborhood-based events outside the walls of the school that help build relationships.
- Family classes related to language, health, wellness, academics, and fun.
- Family members invited to do the morning announcements with their children once or twice a month.

Radical kinship has the potential to lead us to a holistic understanding of who we are in relationship to our community, which supports our ability to create a profound connection between schools and families. Kinship becomes radical when it is reliant on love and encourages us to think differently about existing relations among families, school, students, and community to spur purposeful and meaningful growth.

Question to Consider

- How can you build connections based on the principle of radical kinship within the school–family–community engagement triad?

CULTIVATING THE SOIL: POSSIBILITIES OF DLBE PROGRAMS AS MODELS FOR SCHOOL COMMUNITY

How does a DLBE program avoid the commodification of language and begin to foster a sense of radical kinship? Like a seed needing sustenance, warmth, and time to develop, so too does a transformative school community rooted in kinship. We believe that a DLBE program has the potential to serve as a model for growing such an environment. In its truest form, DLBE programs are as much about cultural competency and inclusive communities as they are about bilingualism (Christian, 1996).

Melanie, Bill, y (and) Mackenzie

Melanie and her husband Bill were from a small community in Tennessee and moved to Virginia prior to their daughter entering school. They were set to enroll in a school that offered a DLBE program. Never having previously heard about such a program, they discussed it and felt it might be a great opportunity for their daughter, Mackenzie. They received a lot of criticism from their extended family for considering such a program, for reasons ranging from academic to political. Ultimately, they proceeded with the application because they wanted their child to have more opportunities than they had ever received.

Melanie felt her upbringing was very homogenous with family members who were extremely prejudiced, and she wanted Mackenzie to be less judgmental and afraid of difference. Bill's motivation was his desire for Mackenzie to become bilingual in order to have better education and job opportunities than he had. Mackenzie's application was chosen in the lottery just weeks before kindergarten began. They nervously accepted the slot.

Immediately, Melanie and Bill could see this program would be different from anything they had experienced. Their child quickly began using words and phrases that they did not know and talked about playdates with kids from Spanish-speaking homes they had never met. Melanie, like many English-speaking parents in DLBE, was motivated at the onset to find ways to be involved and make connections with families to foster her daughter's new friendships; however, she lacked the communication and confidence to proceed. Further, she was afraid of offending because of her lack of cultural understanding. She attended every DLBE event but felt her only ways of showing interest were setting up/tearing down for the event and smiling a lot. Bill tried to take online Spanish classes to help with homework and feel more connected with the Spanish-speaking families. Over time, their enthusiasm for DLBE dwindled and they began to doubt their decision to remain in the program. They felt frustrated with how difficult it seemed to make meaningful connections with families and support Mackenzie's participation in the program.

Earlier in this chapter, we discussed the size of DLBE programs as a challenge because social and linguistic lines tend to be more visible. Yet, if relationships are cultivated using authentic *cariño*, the size becomes an asset for growing organic relationships between and among DLBE families. It is hard to envision opportunities for families to truly connect with one another in a school with a population of 800 students representing more than 30 languages. As a result, family engagement activities continue to remain school-centric, with agendas and/or planning occurring by the school staff and traditional cadre of parents who are considered "involved." We believe DLBE programs (like that of Mackenzie's) can be spaces where schools and families risk being innovative and creative to re-envision more collaborative ties.

In such programs, there are two predominant languages, a small number of families, and hopefully some level of commitment to enhancing cultural understanding since all have agreed (or pushed) to be part of the program. We recognize that piloting creative DLBE family endeavors has the potential to exacerbate negative sentiments of staff and the larger school community who already feel like stepchildren of a school whose focus is the DLBE program. Yet, if handled carefully, it may have quite the opposite effect. Having families work collaboratively with administrators and teachers may help staff realize that re-envisioning family and community engagement is more possible than originally thought. Such attempts could then be modified or expanded to include the greater school community, resulting in a resurgence of enthusiasm from administrators, staff, and families due to observed outcomes from DLBE activities.

Examples of Transformative DLBE Engagement Activities

It has been our experience over the years that in any DLBE program, several English-speaking and CLD families wish for opportunities to connect and understand one another better. For this reason, Lisa Porter (coauthor of this text) and Sylvia Whitney Beitzel (Virginia licensed mediator, interpreter, and homeschool liaison) helped pilot a 5-week DLBE family engagement activity that took place in the same school district Mackenzie attended. The project, *Journeying Together/ Compañeros de camino,* was based on the desire by CLD families and English-speaking parents, like Melanie and Bill, to get beyond the linguistic, cultural, and socioeconomic barriers that limited meaningful interactions between DLBE families.

Families continued to express their desires to have the opportunity to "simply talk and get to know one another's stories." Obviously, this desire presented various possibilities but also required great sensitivity to ensure that families did not feel overly exposed or vulnerable. The agenda for the family-driven project included three specific goals:

1. Establish relations that will build a bridge between native English-speaking and Spanish-speaking families within DLBE program as well as the community at large.
2. Develop a heightened knowledge and appreciation for the cultures and life stories representative of the group.

3. Envision collaboration beyond the seminar for DLBE families through ongoing conversations and exposure to community resources that support intercultural ties.

The project was first piloted in 2016 at one of the four elementary schools in a Virginia school district offering DLBE at that time (Porter, 2018). With the help of DLBE teachers and that particular school's school–home liaison, invitations to participate were shared with the DLBE community. Each participating family was asked to commit to the entire duration of the project (once a week for 5 weeks). The goal was to have 30 of the total 160 DLBE families participate, with 15 from each of the two language groups. Within 2 weeks, 33 families (17 native Spanish-speaking and 16 native English-speaking families) had signed up for the project. Child care, dinner, and materials were provided each week by the school district, with a portion of financial support provided by a small grant received from the Virginia Foundation for the Humanities.

The 5-week seminar was organized thematically with a new topic each week. The topics were derived from conversations with families enrolled in the seminar. The authentic generation of the themes allowed for a flexible structure that enabled families to feel more comfortable interacting with one another as active participants rather than as audience members. Each week, the themes were introduced at the beginning of the session to the entire group and usually included a hands-on activity or demonstration to contextualize meaning. Small breakout sessions would follow for parents to debrief as well as expand on the topic at hand. Parents/caregivers were asked to reflect on their own perceptions and experiences through individual writing activities and personal sharing in small groups. Following breakout sessions, the entire group would reconvene to reflect on the evening before departing.

Because language barriers would pose a significant challenge for meaningful small-group interactions to occur, Porter and Whitney Beitzel decided to reach out to a community partner in an unconventional way. They visited the local state university down the street from the pilot school and asked various programs at the university, including the university's service-learning center, to help recruit six native Spanish-speaking students to volunteer as interpreters for this project. Volunteers who were selected had a vested commitment to the project based on their own experiences in K–12 schools as CLD students. They were required to undergo training and served as table facilitators and interpreters during small-group discussions. The decision to utilize university students rather than DLBE teachers was made in order to provide more open conversations without the interference of formalities or roles typically played by parents and educators. Student volunteers were relatively younger than the parents yet possessed cultural competency in both linguistic worlds as first-generation college students. They had no administrative power in the program or direct connection with the families in the DLBE program. Although attending families expressed no ill feelings toward the DLBE staff, the decision to utilize outside facilitators/interpreters offered a space for families to experience direct contact with one another. Administrators of the school site fully supported the project and came to the beginning of the first session to welcome families and explain that they would not be participating as it was a project/space designed for families to connect.

The first week's theme was titled "The Story of My Name." Cultural emphasis was placed on understanding surnames (traditional order of names in Hispanic cultures as well as choices commonly seen by married individuals in the United States, such as to hyphenate, use spouse's name, or maintain maiden name). Participants were then asked in small groups to share the story behind their first name (or nickname), as a reminder of the value of recognizing one another by name. Families shared stories about changing names, adjusting to mispronunciations, disliking their names, and/or feeling connected to someone they love who was their namesake. Other themes explored during the seminar included respecting commonalities and differences, negative impacts of stereotyping, social norms and feelings of being an insider/outsider, and key components of a collaborative community, including goals for moving forward.

Twenty-six of the 33 families attended the duration of the project. At its culmination, families were given a *Journeying Together/ Compañeros de camino* magazine that included pictures, contact information, quotes, and goals of participants as well as a phone script in English/Spanish for parents to use when arranging a playdate with their children. Although this particular school had explored various engagement activities in the past, there hadn't been an intercultural parent discussion group with topics like those explored in the *Journeying Together/ Compañeros de camino* seminar.

Participants from both language groups indicated on surveys that they found the experience to be extremely beneficial in creating authentic ties within the DLBE community. The consensus was that participants (representing both languages) felt moderately to extremely comfortable at this school and interacting with staff, but admitted to not participating in most school events. One English-speaking parent, whose child had been at the school for 3 years, said that this was the first event he had attended beyond parent–teacher conferences. As a result of school support for the *Journeying Together/Compañeros de camino* seminar, one thing became apparent: Parents wanted meaningful interactions that allowed for dialogue and discovery.

One of the Spanish-speaking participants, for example, shared her appreciation for having a space to talk about her family's story and felt supported and respected in doing so. She said that it "felt nice to have interactions with other parents who were genuinely interested in knowing me and my family's story." Endless comments were made by both sets of parents about initial perceptions and the tendency to make assumptions about those who differ from ourselves. Some families admitted that they had never experienced moments of feeling like an outsider and reflected on the impact this has had on their ways of seeing the world.

Based on the success of the pilot program, the project was modified and replicated at an additional site in the district. Each implementation produced positive feedback from English-speaking and Spanish-speaking participants alike. Various park gatherings, Facebook pages, project reunions, and playdates (including that of Mackenzie and her friend, Alejandra) were the result of this project. The project was not especially grandiose, and it had its flaws. Yet important lessons were learned.

Families generally want to feel a part of a learning community, particularly if they are the navigators of what engagement in this community looks like. This project would not have existed without the desires of families to connect with one another. This project flourished due to the participants as well as the hands-off leadership approach of administration. The administrators at the pilot school (as well as at the additional site) saw the significance of such a program and felt that families needed a space where they could speak freely. The principals at each site found funding for the project, attended the first meeting to demonstrate enthusiasm, and came to the family potluck after the session had ended. Families felt supported but also affirmed in having this time simply to be with one another.

This is a hard paradigm shift for school leaders who feel that if they are not "front and center," things will not go according to plan. Administrators also tend to feel there must be a measurable product or outcome at the end. Granted, "measurements" were facilitated in this case by tracking weekly participant retention and gathering feedback through surveys for funding purposes. However, attendance never became the driving goal or focus of the project. It wasn't about recruiting the largest number of people to attend. The pilot school's administrator was not afraid to try something new. Instead, her response was, "Let's try it. If families find it beneficial, fantastic. If they don't, what is the harm?"

We recognize that at the time this project was piloted, national sentiments and the ability of CLD families to share their stories may have been different than they are today. Yet, even in the current sociopolitical climate, we continue to see the desire for radical kinship from families across the country. Whether it is offering space within the walls of the school or supporting grassroots parent organizations as discussed in Chapter 4, administrators and teachers have the ability to create an atmosphere and energy that is inclusive through supportive servant leadership (Greenleaf, 1991). Seeds for family engagement are planted when trust and respect are demonstrated in small, authentic, and sometimes unconventional ways.

CONCLUSION

In this chapter, we have focused on the unique challenges and opportunities that arise for educators teaching and administering ESL and DLBE programs. We have provided a brief overview of such programs and ways in which bilingual instruction can take an additive or subtractive instructional approach. We have also discussed the possibilities that arise from working with CLD families in smaller settings, such as DLBE programs. Yet DLBE programs that do not prioritize cultural competency through the narratives of families create sociolinguistic divisions that become especially obvious and damaging. DLBE programs can be reduced to a whitewashing version of language learning without cultural context or community collaboration. Alternatively, DLBE programs can be the source of transformative dialogue that provides a foundation for authentic relationship building.

We end the chapter with an example of a piloted program that demonstrated the inherent desire of parents to create a sense of radical kinship within their school community. Sometimes, the key to growing strong relationships is patience and willingness to try something different. What made the *Journeying Together/Compañeros de camino* program successful was not its "wow factor" in bringing in key speakers or offering lots of freebies through raffles. Rather, its effectiveness was situated in the simplicity of meaningful interactions among families that were based on trust and respect. As educators, we need to humbly unlearn our traditional ways of doing and know when to step up or step back.

Check It Out

(Questions to Guide Reflection and Discussion)

1. Critically reflect on the following:
   - Do parent meetings (PTA, etc.) at your school currently reflect the cultural and linguistic diversity of the student population?
   - Do you know the language backgrounds and family narratives of the families you serve?
   - How are cultural narratives woven into current ESL/DLBE instruction and family programming to enhance cultural competency?

Plan It Out

(Creating an Idea That Requires Action)

2. In a team, think and act on the following:
   - Conduct school language inventory walk-throughs with families. In doing this, teachers walk with families through the school and classrooms to identify which labels might need to be changed and determine how languages could be better represented.
   - Set up collaboration structures between educators and with families and community members to create and evaluate curriculum that reflects the biography and narratives of the school's students.

Try It Out

(Attempting Action and Reflecting upon Outcomes)

3. Consider the following:
   - After completing the school language inventory walk-throughs and collaborating with families on curriculum, reflect:
     - ✓ What did you learn from the walk-throughs? What patterns did you find?
     - ✓ What is one example of a curricular change that you made, using insights from families?
   - Identify innovative ways your school might partner with a community organization in creating and funding initiatives that enhance family engagement. Is there an idea like *Journeying Together/Compañeros de camino* to explore?

Momentos de Reflexión (Moments of Reflection)

1. What is something you would like to learn from the families you serve?
2. What has been a memorable teacher/family moment for you? What made it memorable?
3. How does your upbringing enhance or limit your understanding of CLD family narratives?

REFERENCES

Boyle, G. (2017). *Barking to the choir: The power of radical kinship*. New York, NY: Simon & Schuster.

Butler, J. (2002). Is kinship always already heterosexual? *Differences: A Journal of Feminist Cultural Studies, 13*(1), 14–44.

Castañeda v. Pickard, 781 F.2d 456 (1978).

Cervantes-Soon, C. (2014). A critical look at dual language immersion in the Latin@ diaspora. *Bilingual Research Journal, 37*(1), 64–82.

Christian, D. (2006). Two-way immersion education: Students learning through two languages. *The Modern Language Journal, 80*(1), 66–76.

Collier, J. F., & Yanagisako, S. J. (Eds.). (1987). *Gender and kinship: Essays toward a unified analysis*. Berkley, CA: Stanford University Press.

Cummins, J. (1979). Linguistic interdependence and the educational development of bilingual children. *Review of Educational Research, 49*(2), 221–251.

Davidoff, L. (2005). Kinship as a categorical concept: A case study of nineteenth century English siblings. *Journal of Social History, 39*(2), 411–428.

de Jong, E. J., & Harper, C. A. (2005). Preparing mainstream teachers for English-language learners: Is being a good teacher good enough? *Teacher Education Quarterly, 32*(2), 101–124.

ESSA. (2015). Every Student Succeeds Act of 2015, Pub. L. No. 114–95 § 114 Stat. 1177 (2015–2016).

Flores, N., & García, O. (2017). A critical review of bilingual education in the United States: From basements and pride to boutiques and profit. *Annual Review of Applied Linguistics, 37*, 14–29.

Freire, P. (1970). *Pedagogy of the oppressed*. New York, NY: Continuum.

García, O. (2009). *Bilingual education in the 21st Century: A global perspective*. Malden, MA: Wiley-Blackwell.

Greenleaf, R. (1991). *The servant as leader*. Indianapolis, IN: Robert K. Greenleaf Center.

Hayden, C. (2007). Kinship theory, property, and the politics of inclusion: From lesbian families to bioprospecting in a few short steps. *Signs: Journal of Women in Culture and Society, 32*(2), 337–345.

Heller, M. (2010). The commodification of language. *Annual Review of Anthropology, 39*, 101–114.

Izquierdo, E. (2011). Two-way dual language education. In R. Valencia (Ed.), *Chicano school failure and success: Past, present and future* (3rd ed., pp. 160–172). New York, NY: Taylor & Francis.

Lau v. Nichols, 414 U.S. 563 (1974).

Morales, Z., & Maravilla, J. (2019). The problems and possibilities of interest convergence in a dual language school. *Theory into Practice, 58*(2), 145–153.

National Center for Education Statistics. (2016). *The condition of education 2016 (NCES 2016–144), English language learners in public schools*. Washington,

DC: U.S. Department of Education, Author. Retrieved from nces.ed.gov
/fastfacts/display.asp?id=96

Parkin, R., & Stone, L. (2004). *Kinship and family: An anthropological reader.*
Malden, MA: Blackwell.

Porter, L. (2018). Journeying together/Compañeros de camino: Improving
parent relations within dual-language immersion programs as a model
for cross-cultural understanding and collaboration. *Journal of Interdisciplinary Studies in Education, 6*(2), 19–31.

Shenk, M. K., & Mattison, S. M. (2011). The rebirth of kinship: Evolutionary
and quantitative approaches in the revitalization of a dying field. *Human
Nature, 22*(1–2), 1–15.

Thomas, W. P., & Collier, V. P. (2012). *Dual language education for a transformed
world.* Albuquerque, NM: Fuente Press.

Valdés, G. (1997). Dual-language immersion programs: A cautionary note
concerning the education of language-minority students. *Harvard Educational Review, 67*(3), 391–429.

Williams, C. (2017, December 28). *The intrusion of white families into bilingual
schools.* Retrieved from www.theatlantic.com/education/archive/2017/12
/the-middle-class-takeover-of-bilingual-schools/549278

CHAPTER 6

Projecting Our Socialization No Longer

Pobrecitos Hijos y Padres (Pity for Poor Children and Parents)

We are born with dreams in our hearts, looking for better days ahead.

—Jimmy Santiago Baca (1990), p. 12

Key Concepts: socialization, critical reflection, mutual accommodation, meaning perspective

---

INTRODUCTION

As educators, our minds are often consumed with worlds colliding—the complex worlds of each one of our students, those of our administrators and colleagues, our own personal lives and work lives, the turbulent events of our global society—and so many messages received that we cease trying to make sense of where our attitudes and beliefs come from or how they might influence our daily interactions with those around us. We seldom audit the language we use or the messages our words communicate to the world. These words encapsulate many of our thoughts that often remain hidden to us as we make our way. They paint a picture of what K–12 schooling, learning, and family engagement should look like from our perspective. Given the ongoing pressure we face to address low test scores, absenteeism, misbehavior, and other challenges, our default may be to look for who we can blame for the woes that confront us daily in the classroom. Conscious, courageous conversations guided by frameworks that support our reflection

are necessary to begin to audit our thinking about parents/caregivers/
families and the impact their engagement has on us as actors within a
bounded place.

As educators, we have all witnessed the first few weeks of school,
where teachers take on the charge to learn about the families of each
of the learners they are welcoming into their classrooms for the new
year. In elementary grades, the walls are often covered with draw-
ings of pictures of the family. Teachers in upper grades invite family
photographs and writings about the family. Often this is where our
reflections on and valuing of the family begins and ends. Soon our
discourse turns to defining families, parents, and caregivers through
the lens in which we have been socialized. As explained in prior chapters, the organization and norms of schools often reflect the dominant
view of parental engagement, especially: (1) individualism rather than
collectivism (Faitar, 2006); (2) rigid and fossilized school rules and
boundaries (Liddicoat, Scarino, & Kohler, 2018); (3) nuclear notions
of family and parenting (Howard, 2012); and (4) a static conception of
the school's community that reflects its physical location instead of its
potential to foster members' interconnections, sharing, and belonging
(Bower, 2012).

In turn, the school-centric thinking and language that tends to
emerge from these norms often reflects a broad range of assumptions about and judgments of students, families, and communities.
Unfortunately, these culture-bound assumptions typically are unquestioned, unexamined, alienating, and consequential for parent and
community engagement (Herrera & Murry, 2016; Jerald, n.d.; Souto-
Manning & Swick, 2006). Consider the following scenario told by a
university teaching supervisor who had just arrived at an elementary
school to visit her student teachers:

> Recently, I found myself consoling a 2nd-grader who was sitting and
> waiting to the see the principal. I asked him if this beautiful day had some
> bumps along the way. With tears rolling down his boyish face, he looked
> up at me and started to tell me about his mishap. Within a few minutes,
> he was off into the principal's office. It wasn't but a few minutes later
> that I found myself walking down the hall at the same time as the boy I
> had met earlier. He and his teacher had left the principal's office and were
> walking down the hall. I asked, "Rough morning?" The teacher replied,
> "Yes, he's a mess! Doesn't stand a chance this year. Last week his mother
> sent him to school with a sack lunch that consisted of coke, chips, and a
> candy bar. With a parent like that, what can we expect from this child?

Poor kid!" With those comments, she and the boy disappeared into the classroom. I asked myself, "Where to go from there?"

Questions to Consider

- What assumptions has the teacher made about the mother?
- Where did the teacher's immediate reaction come from?
- What expectations are there for the learner, based on the teacher's perception of the mother?
- How did this overheard judgment affect the child?

In the next section, this chapter introduces a framework for holding conversations and assessing our ways of thinking about what is possible with culturally and linguistically diverse (CLD) parents/caregivers. The framework positions educators to critically reflect on what they say and audit the reality of what they do in practice. Only by aligning our beliefs and our practices will we move toward culturally responsive family engagement.

ACCOMMODATION READINESS: SOCIALIZED TO EXPECT

School-centric perspectives about CLD students, families, and communities often operate as unexamined filters influencing how the school–family–community triad is perceived, discussed, and approached (Nelson & Guerra, 2014). The potential contributions of CLD students and caregivers to academic learning and English language acquisition/literacy are often discounted and sometimes completely ignored (Guerra & Nelson, 2011; Hill, Witherspoon, & Bartz, 2018). Students' differences/deviations from the expected school norm are approached as deficits to be corrected or overcome, often through remedial instruction or assistance (Nelson & Guerra, 2014). Such remediation regularly isolates CLD students from the grade-level curriculum and stigmatizes them as *something less*. CLD parents, caregivers, and community members, in turn, are seldom approached as potential resources for learning, teaching, and supporting student success (Herrera, Murry, & Holmes, in press; Hill, Witherspoon, & Bartz, 2018). Instead their racial, cultural, linguistic, and behavioral differences are perceived as contributors to student deficits, barriers to student assimilation, and deterrents to English language acquisition.

An alternative, asset-based perspective on difference is presented by the accommodation readiness spiral (ARS) (Herrera & Murry, 2005, 2016). The ARS encompasses a different view on both the previously mentioned triad and what it means to *accommodate* its members. This framework presents an alternative viewpoint; CLD students and parents/caregivers bring a wealth of assets (versus deficits) to the school and classroom that is too often overlooked or ignored by the school-centric perspective. Accommodation from this viewpoint emphasizes not what CLD students and families don't know, don't have, or don't share or show, but rather the capacities, potentials, and assets they *do* have. Effectively maximizing the assets students and families bring, while attending to their most pressing needs, best reflects the notion of *mutual accommodation* (Arias & Morillo-Campbell, 2008; Espinosa, 2011; Mendenhall, Bartlett, & Ghaffar-Kucher, 2017; Nieto, 1992). Neither unilateral accommodation from the family nor from the school educators is expected. Rather, the goal is to synergize the resources that each brings to the school and classroom.

The spiral, as illustrated in Figure 6.1, offers a heuristic process for educators who wish to reflect on or develop their readiness for the mutual accommodation of CLD students, families, and communities. Foundational to the spiral is Level 1, Readiness for Critical Reflection on Practice. As previously discussed, the socialization patterns of CLD students and families are often different from those of school leaders and educators. This difference frequently initiates assumptions about the CLD triad that too often go unsurfaced, unchecked, and unaddressed. Such assumptions are at the core of teachers' recurrent perceptions that CLD parents don't care about their child's education, don't want to participate in school activities, or are not interested in helping their child complete homework assignments. At the other end of the progression, Level 6 of the ARS represents an educator's readiness for application and advocacy in efforts, for example, to influence and ground in best practice schoolwide approaches to CLD family engagement.

Although each level of the ARS is progressive, the spiral reflects the contingency that regression to a prior level is possible. Critical reflection is pivotal to progression up the spiral; it encourages us to examine the extent to which assumptions about caregivers from another culture are a product of our own socialization (Mezirow, 2007; Murry, 2012). Differences between an educator's espoused and practical readiness for accommodation are illustrated by the double-helix form of the ARS. The structure of the model illustrates the reality that

Figure 6.1. Accommodation Readiness Spiral (ARS)

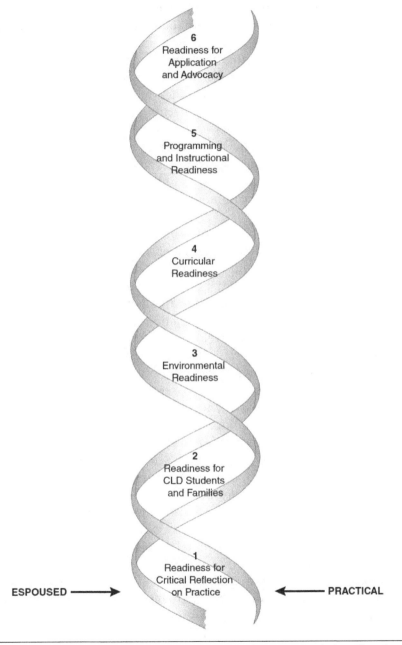

6
Readiness for
Application
and Advocacy

5
Programming
and Instructional
Readiness

4
Curricular
Readiness

3
Environmental
Readiness

2
Readiness for
CLD Students
and Families

1
Readiness for
Critical Reflection
on Practice

ESPOUSED ⟶   ⟵ PRACTICAL

Source: Herrera, Socorro G.; Murry, Kevin G., *Mastering ESL/EFL Methods: Differentiated Instruction for Culturally and Linguistically Diverse (CLD) Students*, 3rd Ed., Figure 5.2, p. 135. Reprinted by permission from Pearson Education Inc., New York, NY.

our actions do not always parallel the beliefs we profess about best practices for the students and families we serve. When these two helices of the ARS are not in sync, our ability to accommodate students and families suffers.

The ARS has the potential to support educators as they begin to explore culturally responsive practices for identifying both the needs and assets of parents/caregivers, families, and the larger community. Key to moving forward is critical reflection on culture-bound beliefs and assumptions about families. We must be willing to redefine our meaning perspectives and meaning schemes associated with the roles of parents, families, and caregivers. What do these roles mean for our daily interactions with CLD learners and those that care for them? How prepared are we to accommodate individuals who are raising the students we teach?

The term *meaning perspective* may be defined as a tacit belief system for the interpretation and evaluation of experiences we have in schools—including those with the families that we serve. They result from life and professional experiences that become so embedded in our ways of thinking and doing that they are often not questioned when we find ourselves in unpredictable situations (Mezirow, 2007). As discussed in Chapter 1, without developing a sociological imagination, the unquestioned assumptions framed within our past lead us to perceive the world through our own unique cultural lens. Meaning systems have the potential to become what we see. They influence how we interpret and evaluate the experiences we have with students and their families. Without our realization, they can have a far-reaching impact on the willingness of both the learner and the parent/caregiver to risk within a system that may prejudge who they are and the community in which they live (Herrera, Holmes, Murry, & Kavimandan, 2019).

Meaning perspectives play out in our practice in unsuspecting ways. They contribute to *whether* and *how* we respond to and utilize new learning through accommodations with our students and families. Over the years, views of parental involvement and engagement have changed very little within our school and classroom context. According to Fernández and López (2017), we continue to premise our ways of thinking about parental involvement in specific, discrete ways that continue to open pathways for the privileged in school contexts, while rendering invisible the funds of knowledge (Moll & González, 2004) of those families we marginalize.

As school demographics have shifted toward increasing student diversity, legislative and policy guidelines increasingly promote higher and more meaningful levels of family engagement in schools and classrooms. Yet the reality is that the meaning perspectives of many school leaders and teachers have changed little in the past 20 or more years (Herrera, Murry, & Holmes, in press). Existing practices with families do little to accommodate new cultures, languages, and perspectives on schooling and education. Parental engagement continues to comprise a set of school-centric activities planned and implemented through the mechanisms described in previous chapters. The language we use is a reminder that deficit thinking still prevails within our system.

These patterns beg the question: What are we doing to enhance our readiness to accommodate CLD student/family needs and assets in ways that are defensible, but may not always feel comfortable or align with school-centric norms? Will we simply espouse our willingness to translate best practices into action with students/families, or will we begin the challenging, but rewarding, process of putting our beliefs into action?

CRITICAL REFLECTION:
FAMILY IS WHERE OUR OWN STORIES BEGIN

Effective capacity building begins with new habits of mind, especially critical reflection on self, on our socialization, and on the congruence of our actions. Each phase of our life—our home (primary socialization), our education (secondary socialization), and ultimately our profession (tertiary socialization)—has a way of "fossilizing" the way we view parents, especially those who are culturally or linguistically different from us. What our meaning perspectives tell us to *expect* from CLD families often contradicts the understandings, collaborations, and successes that are *possible* if we approach families with an unfiltered perspective. At the "gut" level, we frequently revert back to our habits of understanding when confronted with uncomfortable situations. Our responses to parents are reactive, built over years of socialization. Therefore, what we say we want for CLD families often does not occur because we really do not believe it is possible, given their life circumstances. Until we address this discrepancy between what we espouse to be best for families and how we actually perceive, talk about, and attend/accommodate them in our schools, we will not be able to move forward.

Accommodation and new ways of thinking and doing as they relate to building relationships and trust, and thus engaging families, will require developing a capacity for identifying and examining our deeply embedded assumptions about families and the learner. We have to *validity test* the gut reaction we have to the events that happen in students' lives. We often have to risk and challenge the ways of thinking we carry around from our socialization. These processes of identifying and testing the validity of our assumptions, and then locating the source of the assumptions within our own socialization, define what it means to *critically reflect* (Herrera & Murry, 2016). Our daily language is often loaded with judgments about the learners we are teaching, as was true in the short vignette presented at the beginning of this chapter. It is time we develop a new lens for seeing the beauty of what's possible with students and families. The ARS framework can scaffold our thinking about change and our understanding of the types of readiness that can impact our success with parental engagement.

REFLECTION ON THE ARS LEVELS: IMPLICATIONS FOR PARENTAL *CONFIANZA, CARIÑO, Y RESPETO* (TRUST, LOVING CARE, AND RESPECT)

Level 1—Reflection on Self: Shuffling the Deck

Level 1 of the ARS, Readiness for Critical Reflection, asks us to step back and consider the question: Does anyone really choose the cards that he or she is dealt at birth, or the events that unfold throughout life? Do assumptions about the low cards dealt actually benefit the learner or the family? If not, we should ask ourselves: Why do we hold the assumptions we do, and how do we begin to address them?

At the philosophical core of the ARS is the educator's decision to be honest. We must be honest about the assumptions and language we use to describe *why* a student acts, learns, or behaves in certain ways in the classroom. Rarely have we sufficiently reflected on the influence that *the source* has on our capacities to teach the child who may come from a "less-than-desirable" family context. The journey of letting go of our assumptions begins with building a capacity for first examining our assumptions and testing how valid they really are. We then examine our own life experiences and expectations, given our socialization in a particular culture. Through such self-directed and honest reflection, we begin to understand why we hold certain beliefs about the families we serve. We begin to see why we pass judgment on the mother who sends her child to school without a coat, lunch, or homework completed, and many more school-centric ways of thinking and doing. Consider the following narrative from a teacher:

> I cringe every time I see George's father come into the school and I secretly send out a wish to the universe that he not come into my classroom or that I'm not in the office so I don't have to talk to him. I prefer he talks to the paraprofessional. I think they both live in the neighborhood. It's just that I hear he's been in prison for drug use and dealing. I have not had to deal with anyone like that. It gives me an uneasy feeling to have to be face to face with someone who just got out of prison. My neighborhood is not like that.

This type of narrative is often expressed in schools about parents' life circumstances. When parents are in the school and we walk down the opposite hall because they do not speak our language, have made choices in life that we do not understand, or are just different enough in background that they make us uncomfortable, we have acted on our assumptions. *Assumptions are the death of all that is possible with students and families.* Our pathways to engagement begin with our first walking beside and learning about the parents/caregivers and families we *serve*. Questions to ask ourselves include:

1. Did I respond to the situation/event from my own way of thinking on how things should be addressed/handled?
2. What feelings (gut level sensations) were experienced? Did I project my own socialized ways of responding onto the situation?
3. When I really think about it (versus feel), how much do I know about the history of the individuals involved in the situation?
4. Am I making any assumptions? Can I name them?
5. Is the event/situation harmful to the learner or others in the class?
6. Are there factors that I may need to consider, in order to explore alternative explanations?
7. After examining my assumptions, did I find that they were valid? If so, how might I move forward in positive, supportive ways? If not, how can I change my approach to this situation, and others like it, in my professional practice?

As educators, our ability to unpack and understand our socialization and the influence it has on how we perceive the complex biography of the learner (including the sociocultural, linguistic, cognitive, and academic dimensions) is key to our success with CLD students and families. How we interpret learning and behavior in classroom practice will greatly influence how we view a student's family and community. Remember, just like each of us educators, each *student* has a story that begins with the context in which he or she has been socialized. Although this context influences the learner's current realities, it neither defines nor determines the potential and possibilities for that learner.

Level 2—Reflection on Families and Students: Deficit or Potential

Level 2 of the ARS is also fundamental to our work. The lens many educators have used to describe, define, and discipline students (especially those who are CLD) has been tied to their own internal socialization monitor. Too often (as discussed in Chapter 2), teachers' language about students who are different is so filled with deficit vernacular (e.g., low SES, at risk, NES, LEP) that their words become a self-fulfilling prophecy. For such educators, students' likely trajectories spawn undesirable conclusions, reflected in sentiments such as, "He's not worth my time. Her story is already written. Neither he nor his parents care— Why should I?" Much about a student's life trajectory is in the hands of teachers and school leaders. Every juncture along the path of CLD students' education may prove either an opportunity to build new bridges, connections, and possibilities, or an indiscriminate force that seeks to erase the family/caregiver-constructed biography of language, experiences, and knowledge that the students already bring to school. Teachers' meaning perspectives come to define and delimit not just students' horizons, but the pathways for providing caregivers with hope in the school's intentions and invitations to engage or collaborate.

At this level of the ARS, the development of appropriate readiness for CLD students and families often depends on our willingness and persistence to seek a deeper understanding of both the learner and his or her caregiver, family, or extended family. This process commonly requires us to critically reflect on the language that is imposed/used by society in reference to CLD communities and families regarding, for example, their immigration status, socioeconomic levels, education levels, and employment (Fernández & López, 2017; Nelson & Guerra,

2014). Such validity testing of this language may lead us to realize that we often jump onto this moving train of deficit thinking without reflecting on the unique perspectives and life experiences of each family.

We may find that when it comes to engaging CLD families, the most difficult type of critical reflection is connected to our meeting family members where they are and walking beside them as they cross the bridge into an unknown and sometime hostile system that may not genuinely understand their life circumstances. We educators would do well to remember the adage against judging others until we have walked no short distance in their shoes. Proving *ready* for meaningful family engagement comes when we truly collaborate in finding new paths and contexts that, for both students and families, intrigue learner interest, connect curricula with biography, and affirm individual worth, knowledge, skills, and capacities.

Fundamentally, the first two levels of the spiral serve as the foundation that informs what we plan for and how we contextualize what we teach inside the classroom, as well as what we build and aspire to achieve with stakeholders outside the school. Our environment, curriculum, instruction, programming, and ultimately how we advocate for our students must be well grounded in the first two levels of the ARS. Without critical reflection and an openness to self-assess our understanding of the parent/caregiver/family with a critical lens, our preparation for meaningful family engagement will prove woefully inadequate.

Level 3—Critical Reflection as Pivotal to a Proactive Environmental Audit

Our work revolves around two distinct environments that impact and inform our classroom. The first environment can be thought of as the physical space in which we teach. This space sends powerful messages about the community that learns there. The second encompasses the milieu of external influences on our pedagogy, curricula, school, and community (Herrera & Murry, 2016). To fully examine this level of the ARS, we as educators must critically reflect on how our classroom environment represents what we believe about CLD students and the power of internal and external influences to propel or impede their linguistic and academic success.

External to our classroom there exists a rich tapestry of community and family dynamics that are far too often not represented on the walls of either our classrooms or our school. In what ways do our lesson plans, materials, and products elicit and express the funds of knowledge (Moll & González, 2004) that students contribute to classroom discourse, interactions, and learning? Are caregivers actively encouraged and enabled to be contributors to classroom lessons, from the perspective of their funds of knowledge? In what ways? Are students' biographies and assets part of the fabric of teaching and learning in the classroom? Such questions and their answers can help us think about our classroom as an ecology for sharing, learning, and producing outcomes indicative of our community that are multicultural, multilingual, and liberatory.

Take a moment to read and reflect on the following narrative from a parent:

> *Señora, ¿Por qué los maestros no me entienden?* (Mrs., why do the teachers not understand me?) I cannot contribute to what they want from me. You see, I'm not educated. I only went to school for 3 years. Now I'm here with my six babies. I want for them what I didn't have: a good education. I want them to not work hard. I want them to not be worried. But all the teacher does is ask me to do work I don't know how to do. *Me da tristeza con lo que me piden.* (I feel embarrassed by what they ask from me.) *Me siento sola.* (I feel alone.) I ask them every day: "How is my son behaving at school?" They respond with, "Help him with his work." All I have to give is to make sure he is a good boy. That is all. I cannot give them any more—just what I know to do: make my boy be good in school. *Quiero que sea educado.* (I want him to be well educated.) *Eso fue lo que me dejaron mis padres.* (That is what my parents left for me.) *Ser una buena persona en este mundo.* (To be a good person in this world.) *De allí más no puedo.* (Beyond that I cannot give anymore.) *Pero eso es importante, ¿verdad?* (Yet, that is important, right?)

Questions to Consider

- From the perspective of parental engagement, what can be learned from this mother's sadness?
- What funds of knowledge might we better articulate by engaging in a conversation with her?
- What have we learned about the external environment of this child?
- Why would knowledge of the external environment matter in the schooling and classroom practices for this student?

The environment that is external to the classroom offers abundant wealth if we as educators are willing to truly embrace a humanitarian view of those we teach and the resources that are already an asset of their culture. The mother in the example wants her child to be *bien educado*, which, at a humanistic level, means to engage with the world in a respectful, loving, and productive way. If she can contribute this to her child, she will continue what her parents provided her. She believes this will build a solid foundation from which her child's teachers, in turn, can build to fulfill the abundance of her potential. The question becomes: How might our internal environment of the classroom engage those funds of knowledge to accommodate the family? For example, how might we use our knowledge of the family to reframe our models of instruction, classroom management, and use of resources?

The internal classroom environment speaks volumes about the way we engage parents within our practice. It sends powerful messages to parents, students, and those who walk the school halls about what matters and how we use the language, parental contributions, and insights into CLD students' funds of knowledge during learning. The internal environment in today's schools typically is dynamic, complex, and complicated to navigate. Sometimes it may feel overwhelming to make sense of it all and still have time to teach. Yet we have to ask: How does what family members have to offer matter in this enterprise we call education? Is it possible that when we value and use what CLD students and families bring, we actually make learning easier and our own teaching more effective? Reflect on the three artifacts in Figure 6.2. What do they say about the internal environment of the classroom? Of the school?

Questions to Consider

- What can be gleaned from each artifact in Figure 6.2?
- How might our new insights help us use the funds of knowledge to build relationships?
- Which artifact(s) have more power for engaging parents?
- In what ways is each artifact an affirmation to the family, caregiver, or learner?

Our preparation for making environmental accommodations that reflect and engage the parent/caregiver/family requires our thinking outside the box and moving beyond the traditional: international nights,

Figure 6.2. Learning About Families: Examples in Practice

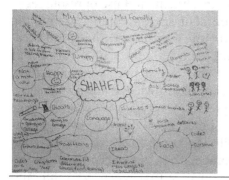

school barbeques, and other point-in-time events that do not inform in-struction and become simply events to attend. Instead, culturally respon-sive and sustainable accommodations are informed by the learners, the families, and their funds of knowledge, and they have well-articulated purposes. Think about the learner who has a father who works at the local dairy and what he or she can contribute based on dinner table con-versations. What about the child whose parent works at the local beef packing plant, or the mother who takes care of senior citizens? How will you harvest the wealth in your classroom, and in your school? We all have cultural capital/wealth. How will the external environment be represented in the hallways and classrooms of your school?

Level 4—Readiness for Dismantling the Curricular Machine

At this level of the spiral, our intent is questioned: Do our ener-gies move us toward learning about parents/caregivers/families to *challenge and transform* our curriculum to better address CLD students? Core to many school mission statements is a vision to provide an equitable learning space for all who attend, regardless of race, ethnicity, language, religion, or sexual orientation. Yet most schools continue to purchase curricula that are heavily marketed and purported to increase reading and math achievement, without reflecting on how the learner and family are represented within. By representation, we are not talking about a few highlighted stories or pictures reflecting the diversity found in classrooms across the United States.

Instead, at the normative level, we are talking about a deep dive into understanding the learners we teach and how the parent/caregiver/family will be able to support the child linguistically and academically to make sense of the topics/content found in the curriculum. Have we ever asked how the community in which our students live enters into the learning picture? How do the stories, activities, and pictures of our curriculum represent the local community? The families? In what ways do our current curricular materials support the parent/caregiver/family in making connections to the content? If the curriculum does not represent the community and family, who will do the work of making adaptations to align it with the wealth/funds of knowledge present in the teaching and learning context? In other words, how will we bring the life/lived experiences of the parent/caregiver/family into the classroom to build an equitable and culturally responsive learning community? Think about the following experiences relayed by one of the authors:

> As a mother of four, I have personally witnessed and questioned the 8th-grade science curriculum used with each of my children who attended the same school across a span of 28 years. For my oldest who is now 40 to my youngest who is 13, the project of the family tree has been emotionally devastating. Here are their stories.
>
> When my oldest daughter was in the 8th grade, she was asked to complete a family tree. At that time, she was living with her stepfather (who she considered more like a father) and me. Attempting to complete the family tree, she struggled. She understood the objective was to trace your genetic lineage and know your history, but in her adolescent mind, she was "cheating" the person raising her. The assignment didn't make sense. Given the way it was presented, she struggled to

see the relevance of this "family" tree. The assignment was not something that she considered necessary to the objective of the lesson, since it was completed in isolation from the readings and other activities that were part of the week. She complied, however, and reluctantly handed in the assignment.

Fast forward 5 years later—same teacher, different child. My son was assigned the task of filling out the family tree. Like his sister, he failed to see the need for this childish activity that had not been presented in a way that made sense to him, given his definition of family. He had very little contact with his biological father and he ignored the completion of the assignment, calculating that it would not bring down his overall grade. I learned of his zero on the assignment at parent–teacher conferences, but left it alone, given the drama with his sister on the same assignment years earlier.

Fifteen years later, my third child—same school, different teacher—gets the same assignment. It's the family tree activity all over again. This time, however, for this child who is adopted, it becomes such an emotional activity that he shuts down; he attends the class, but does not engage. His grade reflects his lack of engagement and motivation. In conversation, I ask, "What happened? This was your favorite class." He responds by sharing a few choice words about how out of touch the teacher is, asking him to do a family tree. "Doesn't he know that I'm adopted? The assignment is totally meaningless, because I have no family! I don't know where I come from. How am *I* supposed to do this meaningless assignment? I would rather be a dropout," he tells me. We never moved forward. That was the end of that!

Now, just a few months into the school year, the family tree project appears again. This time, my baby, who is also adopted, goes into a rant. She tells me, "Who are these people teaching? How am I supposed to do this assignment? I have a biological mother in the mountains somewhere. I don't know who my father is. So, I GUESS, I don't have a history! Who am I? I am not putting you and Dad as my family tree. You two would not count on the rubric. You are not my REAL history." The intuitive, compassionate side of this child then shows through. As tears fill her eyes, she says, "Doesn't this teacher know that Josh, Danielle, and Mark are in foster care. They want to forget their parents. They can't go home and make a pretty tree. Their branches are broken! My branches are a hybrid. The trunk doesn't match the branches and leaves. And then my friend, Leticia, never had a father. Her mom doesn't know who he is" . . . and she proceeds to rant. In her voice I hear the anger and frustration of a teenage girl who is channeling all the histories of one classroom into the pain she is feeling.

Questions to Consider

- During your planning, do you critically reflect on how the curriculum and activities will be interpreted by the learner?
- How do you use what you know to build classroom community and relationships and attend to the socioemotional dimension of the learner?
- How do you document and use what you know about the funds of knowledge and experiences of parents/caregivers/families to guide lesson planning and delivery?

The narrative surrounding the family tree activity raises a variety of questions pertinent to curricular issues. Given the histories of the parents/caregivers/families and the complexity of the community and home realities of the learners, why weren't curricular implications more thoughtfully examined? Twenty years ago, in a west Texas classroom, being from a divorced family was an exception. Today, the diversity of our classrooms demands more thorough examinations of potential implications for learners, such as those who bring varying family structures and realities. The socioemotional pain/damage we as educators can unknowingly inflict in our classrooms is born out of our drive to teach the curriculum, without appropriate levels of attention to the learners and families who will be affected.

Our instruction is greatly influenced by the latest trends in professional development, large corporations that develop one-size-fits-all programming and instructional guidelines/protocols designed to assert uniformity, and norms that place all parents/caregivers/families in the same box. Culturally sensitive and responsive school educators have a professional responsibility to take back the curriculum and design and deliver instruction that is purposefully and defensibly grounded in the realities of classroom learners and the caregivers of the school's community.

Level 5—Readiness to Step Out of the Instructional Box

Increasingly, the literature and realities of the field bemoan the erosion of teacher voice in decisions about what they teach, how they teach, and the outcomes they hope to attain. Too often the focus of corporate-driven curricula and instruction overwhelmingly prioritizes uniformity, compliance, and fidelity. Teachers maintain that they have little volition in responding to students' cultures, languages, biographies, and outcomes. They often feel paralyzed in their efforts to make the sorts of changes they know are necessary to foster academic achievement and English language literacy among CLD and other students.

It is not altogether surprising then, that much of today's learning for students surrounds drill and practice for standardized assessments, sterile curricula, and mountains of worksheets. Instructional planning rarely considers students' biographies, culturally responsive methods and strategies, ways to engage CLD families in support of learning, and affirmation of students' culture-bound ways of knowing. Instead, deficit perspectives prevalent in instruction and curricula consistently and detrimentally center on identification and correction of what is perceived as *wrong* with students and families (Hill, Witherspoon, & Bartz, 2018; Kressler & Cavendish, 2019; Nelson & Guerra, 2014). Consider the following scenario.

> Recently a group of teachers sat around discussing what would be a good way to get parents in this predominantly Latino community involved. The discussion soon became heated between the teachers and the paraprofessionals who were invited to provide information about the community, since most of them lived there. The teachers were concerned that parents were not returning homework, were not accessible when there was a problem, and had such low levels of education that they were a roadblock to their children being successful in learning to read. The suggestion was made that maybe the mothers could come in once a week and watch the teacher model a read aloud with the kids. The paraprofessional would then provide a mini-lesson on how the mothers could take the information and use it to support their child.
>
> At the end of the meeting, it was decided there were too many reasons why this idea would not work. Although it had been a good idea, the teachers concluded that, given the

mothers' levels of education, the risk of them showing up with their other children was too great. The teachers also were concerned about not wasting time. It was best, in the end, to "just do what they could with these kids."

Questions to Consider

- What assumptions did the teachers in the scenario make about instructional possibilities?
- How has the instructional program defined what is possible for the engagement of the parents/caregivers/families?
- In what ways are the meaning perspectives of the educators circumscribing the nature and degree to which the family is involved with instruction?

The meaning perspectives we hold related to the capacities of families are constrained often by programs and instruction that define the limits of our professional practice. Educators frequently—through unwillingness, fear, or lack of awareness of the urgency—*fail to risk*. Imagine the possibilities! Take time to recognize the patterns, challenge the mandates, become knowledgeable about the people who most influence how learners make sense of instruction, and explore how they fit within the program.

Level 6—Readiness to Put Caring into Action

Ultimately, educators' ability to reframe their language and thinking outside of the deficit messages that get passed along in schools is a function of their willingness to critically reflect on such messages and exercise the creativity necessary to be even *subversive* about praxis. It's important to remember that none of us is alone on this journey. With an honest and ongoing commitment to self-reflection, critical thinking, and cross-cultural understanding, teachers will find that CLD families and communities are often ready, willing, and able to join the cause.

Revitalizing our teaching and parent/caregiver/family engagement will necessitate some changes. We must:

- Critically examine and recognize the influence of our own socialization in how we approach students and caregivers.
- Let go of deficit thinking.

- Take time to know our students and their biographies.
- Approach caregivers and families as assets to our advocacy and creativity.
- Prioritize instruction that is biography driven and culturally responsive.
- Affirm students' successes, however small, as well as our own independence as well-educated, caring professionals.

It's often difficult to envision ourselves as advocates or activists. After all, marching in the streets is not something that we have been prepared to do. Our college courses likely did not prepare us for even the simpler roles we can play within the more manageable contexts of our own classrooms, schools, and communities. Yet, it is within each of us as educators. It's what caring and doing the right thing is all about. Consider the far-reaching effects of fear in the following narrative from a teacher:

> There are times I just want to go out into the community and join the families in asking questions—let them know not to be afraid of the knocking on doors. I know sometimes they fear the system, us, because they are not documented. But it's not only our undocumented families that don't ask questions, it's all families. Our school seems to only want parents to bring the cupcakes and Kleenex, be present for the parties, and do homework with their kids. I want more, but I don't have the tools. No one has prepared me for advocacy. I live in fear of alienating my colleagues, or even worse, losing my job.

Questions to Consider

- What are the assumptions embedded in this teacher's language?
- To what degree does her thinking about the school's openness to parents/caregivers/families reflect the administrators and teachers at your school?
- Is advocacy for learning about families a teacher's responsibility? Why or why not?

As we noted, advocacy for parents/caregivers/families is seldom addressed in teacher preparation programs. Few recipes and fewer theories exist for how to make it a habit of the job. Yet, we have argued in this text that our interactions with CLD families and caregivers are great places to begin learning what advocacy means, and what it takes to make it a reality in our daily practice. Teachers already know much about making a case, framing a persuasive argument, grounding their position in the literature, and caring about students and families. To take the next steps, we need to be honest with ourselves and with the system, vulnerable in our willingness to listen and learn from families, and strategic in our efforts to transform instruction and classrooms into sites of responsiveness and authentic care.

REWRITING THE NARRATIVES:
OWNING OUR HISTORICAL REALITY

As authors, our research and conversations with colleagues across the United States have reminded us that there is a paucity of literature that moves beyond an all-too-familiar narrative. Only recently has research started to problematize the paradigms behind the concepts of parental involvement and engagement. Fernández and López (2017) state: "Indeed, the discourse surrounding parental involvement has recently undergone a shift that has problematized the structures and ideologies that perpetuate a homogenized and simplified understanding of parental involvement" (p. 115). To understand why parents/caregivers/families continue to be marginalized and bound by a deficit perspective, individuals must understand their own socialization within an educational *system* that is afraid of opening its doors to difference.

Together, we must work to dismantle the "fossilized" research, definitions, and practices that have continued to drive our narrative. Questions must be raised about educators' meaning perspectives—the stories we tell ourselves about the world and how it works, based on the experiences or knowledge we have gained throughout our life. We must shed light on how school-centric definitions undergird a silencing of possibilities for parents who do not fit the cultural norms and frames of reference of the dominant culture. Our meaning perspectives become our reality, and they have the potential to paralyze our action toward advocacy.

Personal and Professional Dissonance

According to Lightfoot (1978), our focus on role construction for parents may lead to a context of "blaming cycles" between teachers and parents. Though often well intended, such meaning perspectives may, in the end, be hurtful to all parties involved. Included in this section are voices from longitudinal research (Herrera, 1995; Morales, Abrica, & Herrera, 2019) and current research literature (Lawson, 2003) that provide us with narratives that reflect common themes. The language requires us, as caring professionals, to critically reflect on the origins of these attitudes and beliefs. What do these voices say? What role does our socialization play in creating these narratives? How do we go about redefining current conceptualizations of parental engagement and addressing the deficit perspectives we may hold about communities and families? If parents are the link to academic success, then how does the current blaming narrative influence possibilities for building bridges between community, home, and school?

Think about how the voice of this teacher may prevent the formation of a parent–teacher relationship:

> What has happened to these kids? Some of them are already through with us! They're 7th- and 8th-graders and they've already had enough. It's too late to get them back. That's what is expected of them. Their home life is a wreck. Their parents just don't care! Have you ever seen them attend even one school event?

The voice of this middle school teacher reflects (and simultaneously constructs) a perceived reality about the relationship between her Mexican American students' home environment and parents, and what is possible for achieving success with her student population. Stating that the situation is beyond her control sends the message that reaching out is futile. There is not much that can happen for these students because, after all, the parents "don't care."

Research has found that current school-centric models of parental engagement often serve to perpetuate views that go unquestioned about why Latinx and Black parents may not be responsive to teachers (Durand & Secakusuma, 2019; Fernández & López, 2017; Herrera, 1995; Lawson, 2003; Lopez, 2001; Lopez, Scribner, & Mahitivanichch, 2001; Morales et al., 2019; Williams & Sánchez, 2012). The casualties of deficit or school-centric thinking become the children, adolescents, and young adults in the classroom. Limiting ways of thinking often set the stage for prebounding our contact with parents and for scapegoating, both at the individual and collective level. Our personally constructed beliefs often become group consensus through messages sent during professional development, data-driven meetings, and planning of activities that ask for parent volunteers.

Teachers frequently talk about opening pathways for contacting and engaging parents, yet they tend to place boundaries on the potential for such contact by finding factors or contingencies that justify not following through. Most often teachers talk about having more contact with parents who are not involved or engaged in the more school-centric types of activities. Suggestions abound related to more home visits, more communication via a phone call, and possibly community-based activities; rarely do they encompass nontraditional avenues for engaging parents in ways that are respectful of their current circumstances. Following is an example of a typical perspective on parental engagement from an administrator:

> Our relationship with our families truly needs to be a one-to-one relationship. Another way to build positive relationships with our families beyond phone call communication could be home visits . . . as we all know parents are key to better learning environments in the classroom.

Yet, as authors, we have found from our work with schools that the discourse toward pushing alternative ways of reaching out to parents quickly turns to questions of *whose* responsibility will this be? Maybe it is the responsibility of school liaisons—after all, that's part of their job description; they speak the language and already have had direct contact with families. Or maybe it's the role of the academic team, since they are the ones responsible for grades and decreasing drop-out rates. Often by the end, the conversations turn into a consensus that these types of activities may be beyond the scope of what is possible for the classroom teacher, there are too many obstacles with these particular parents, and communication may prove too difficult. Consider how this line of thinking is exhibited in the following narrative from a teacher:

> Communicating with this parent may prove to be counterproductive! I hear that calling her mother will only create new problems for her. We never know how these parents will respond to us when we reach out. This may be more of a problem than we want to deal with at this time. It's best we keep our communication in written form.

As educators, we sometimes question why we should really put ourselves out there. However, those educators who take ownership to leave the safe spaces often designated for parents (e.g., conferences, meetings, and typical engagement activities) to reinvent new ways of attending to, communicating, and learning about families redraw the lines for what is possible.

For teachers who do consider the benefits of making home visits (Peck & Reitzug, 2018), their conversations frequently are bound by issues surrounding feasibility, and their thinking is often rooted in perspectives of fear of the unknown. Home visits quickly become an unmanageable task due to time, fear of personal injury, fear of rejection, or fear of reprisal from administration. Following is an excerpt from a conversation among teachers on why home visits are simply not feasible for them:

> There lies the root of the problem. The parents who need to be the most involved in this school are the most unable to be or are intimidated or for whatever the reason . . . the least involved. Probably the reason their children . . . are already struggling in school is the lack of emphasis placed on the value of education. . . . Home visits to all these homes to prompt involvement is not feasible.

What we as educators choose to know about parents and home environments serve as a selective consciousness that supports teachers' interpretations and ideologies about CLD students and their parents.

Letting Go: Participatory Practices for Equal Partnership

Moving forward means letting go of the prevalent (and historically "safe") deficit thinking about learners and their parents. "Pobrecitos" is a term often used in the Spanish language to pity the circumstances of another. Too often in school hallways, meetings, and classrooms, the language used to describe parents and their children is "poor _____," followed by pity about their life circumstances. This language has the potential of closing the door to possibilities, ascribing roles to the actors, and limiting alternative ways of understanding and responding to the situation.

In Lawson's (2003) study, the parents were constantly seeking ways to communicate their lived experiences in the community with the teachers of their children. The parents' ultimate goal was that, by means of their open sharing and communication, the lives of their children would be improved. Yet closed minds and pathways in school-centric ways of viewing parental engagement are operationalized in a "what's-in-it-for-the-system" way of thinking. The parents in Lawson's study knew they were in the fight of their lives for the future of their children.

Research is replete with examples of teachers' meaning perspectives that attribute many of their learners' behaviors, learning disabilities, academic struggles, and challenges in life to the students' homes and community (Durand & Secakusuma, 2019; Lawson, 2003). Often these meaning perspectives are without foundation, since the teacher seldom attends community activities or encounters the parent/caregiver/family in daily interactions in the community (e.g., shopping, church services), and has rarely, if ever, communicated with those closest to the students. Moving forward will take a reconceptualization of what it means to engage parents—and in what spaces and for what purposes.

At the heart of engaging, building trust, and creating a space of mutual respect is understanding that regardless of where we come from, no one can judge us. If others do, we should afford their judgment no credibility. Why? Because no one else knows the struggles we have overcome, nor the aspirations we have for ourselves or for our children. The aspirations we hold for ourselves as parents and the hopes and dreams we hold for our students play out in many different ways. We as authors find through our work that all parents seek to do what's best for their children, and they do the best they can at the moment. Unfortunately, life circumstances are sometimes cruel and do not afford us all the same opportunities (Herrera, 2010, 2016).

To know parents/caregivers/families, one must begin by learning about their biography. This will take engaging in conversation without judgment of one another. In schools and classrooms, this will not occur without critical reflection on the part of those who make up the system that defines the roles for both educator and parent. What if there were no defined roles? What if each individual entered into conversation from a learning perspective that recognized *understanding* as a journey? Deeply embedded assumptions would be checked at each point of contact. According to Durand and Secakusuma (2019), misperceptions and misunderstandings between teachers and parents are never a one-way street. Both parties bring with them a history of experiences that play out within that first point of contact, during which judgments are made about the relationship. However, as educators we have been asked to check our habits of mind. We know the destination we want to reach—the charge is in our hearts to create a third space (Gutiérrez, 2008; Gutiérrez, Baquedano-López, & Tejeda, 2003; Moje et al., 2004) of possibilities with what we learn about our students' community, homes, and families.

A principal recently shared that, for her, the exchange with parents was very seldom about schooling or their children. Every exchange started with a story about news in the community, uneventful chit chat about inconsequential matters. She sought out parents in grocery stores, laundromats, parks, churches—anywhere she might be able to engage authentically. Over time, she found that caregivers and parents started to seek her out at school. Once a relationship had formed where she was perceived as a *person*, not an authority to be feared, but an adult with similar life experiences and interests, the conversations relevant to school followed. Through an approach that was based on empathy, trust, relationship building, and shared humanity, the parents' anxiety, frustration, intimidation, and fear toward the school disappeared.

For the principal, letting go of deficit perspectives she held about families was the first step toward respecting the adults that were doing the best they could in often very difficult life situations. The educators in her school began to let go of system-prescribed ways of thinking about parental involvement, and their definition of engagement transformed. Parental engagement was no longer about parents (1) adhering to the responsibility of facilitating learning at home, (2) attending parent–teacher conferences, (3) serving on decisionmaking committees, or (4) helping out at cultural activities or parent literacy education training. Engagement was no longer defined by dominant cultural norms and frames of reference that were so limiting, given the context in which she led and her teachers taught.

CONCLUSION

Current conversations in the literature ask for recognition of racial and cultural issues in our work as educators. The call is for equity, trust, respect, and an asset-based approach to engaging with parents/

caregivers/families. This type of transformation requires a reconceptu-alization and reconstruction of our thinking and action. It will mean letting go of stereotypes, myths, meaning perspectives, and societal messages about the communities we serve. As with any context, every family has its own sociocultural map filled with struggles, memories, hopes, and dreams for the future. Schools are the catalyst for collabo-ration in forging—sometimes against the tide—new destinations of possibilities. The wonder of this work we carry out as educators is that we weather many storms, but are blessed with so many rainbows, all in a single day's work.

Following are action items for consideration:

1. Plan schoolwide activities that have been framed around what you know about the community (e.g., the music, food, games, and books used at home). Provide a space to have students and families teach the teacher.
2. Keep a bank of family workplaces and align them with the curriculum. Bring in pictures, stories, and artifacts that show students that every job in the community is important.
3. Reach out to families to learn about the activities (e.g., Lotería [Mexican Bingo]) in which they participate with their children and bring those into the school context.
4. Send home "homework" or activities that have multiple points of entry. Make it possible for *every* child to be successful!
5. Engage in conversations about the world, nation, state, and community. Create spaces where human relationships can grow.
6. Let go of what has been and begin to think of *what could be.*

Creating an ecology of mutual respect in which all dimensions of the environment and actors within the space are interconnected is critical to growing as a collective school community. Collaboration begins with gathering all the threads to move in the direction of imag-ining a third space (Gutiérrez, 2008; Gutiérrez et al., 2003) where knowledge is shared and interwoven. All the trainings, standards, in-terventions, multicultural books, apps, and "stuff" that seem to chan-nel our energy and drive our teaching will not get us as far as we can go if we work toward creating new worlds derived from *all* contribu-tions, from every member of the community, including those who share the same physical space as well as those who share our students' hearts.

Check It Out
(Questions to Guide Reflection and Discussion)

1. Reflect on the types of family engagement activities used in your setting of professional practice:
   - Make a list of the current activities that engage your parents/caregivers at each level:
     - ✓ Classroom
     - ✓ Schoolwide
     - ✓ Districtwide
   - How are families' ways of knowing and doing considered during the planning of these various activities?
   - What are the characteristics of parents/caregivers most likely to participate in each activity?
   - What might keep some parents/caregivers from participating?

Plan It Out
(Creating an Idea That Requires Action)

2. In a team, think and act on the following:
   - Discuss each school activity you listed. How could the activity be reframed to get more engagement from those who participate?
   - Make a list of alternative activities that reflect, and could be planned according to, an asset-based perspective.

Try It Out
(Attempting Action and Reflecting upon Outcomes)

3. Think about this chapter and reflect on the levels of the ARS (see next page).
   - As you begin re-imagining new ways to respond with increased readiness, write on the left-hand side of each level one idea you believe is possible for engaging parents. On the right-hand side, add what you would do in practice to turn the idea into reality.

Momentos de Reflexión (Moments of Reflection)

1. In what ways has my socialization influenced my typical actions/reactions in accommodating parents/caregivers/families?
2. How will I make critical reflection on the assumptions I hold and the language I use central to my efforts to re-envision parental engagement?
3. How will I adjust my ways of doing to ensure all parents are treated in an equitable way?
4. How can I better ensure that my relationships with students and their families reflect trust and empathy?

Planning Family Engagement with the Accommodation Readiness Spiral

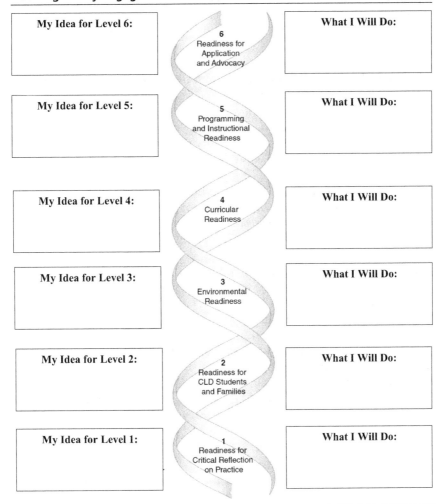

Source: Adapted from Herrera & Murry, 2016, Figure 5.1, p. 135

REFERENCES

Arias, M. B., & Morillo-Campbell, M. (2008). *Promoting ELL parental involvement: Challenges in contested times* (Policy brief). Retrieved from cdr.lib.unc.edu/concern/dissertations/9880vr93j

Baca, J. S. (1990). Immigrants in our own land. In J. S. Baca, *Immigrants in our own land & selected early poems* (pp. 12–13). New York, NY: New Directions Publishing.

Bower, H. A. (2012). *It's all about the kids: School culture, identity, and figured worlds* (Unpublished doctoral dissertation). University of North Carolina, Chapel Hill. Retrieved from cdr.lib.unc.edu/concern/dissertations/9880vr93j

Durand, T. M., & Secakusuma, M. (2019). Negotiating the boundaries of parental school engagement: The role of social space and symbolic capital in urban teachers' perspectives. *Teachers College Record, 121*(2).

Espinosa, S. M. (2011). *Beyond resiliency: Using youth participatory action research to examine alternative education and identity in a high poverty town* (Unpublished doctoral dissertation). University of Massachusetts, Boston.

Faitar, G. M. (2006). Individualism versus collectivism in schools. *College Quarterly, 5*(4), 15–26.

Fernández, E., & López, G. R. (2017). When parents behave badly: A critical policy analysis of parent involvement in schools. In M. D. Young & S. Diem (Eds.), *Critical approaches to education policy analysis: Moving beyond tradition* (Education, Equity, Economy series, Book 4, pp. 111–129). Cham, Switzerland: Springer.

Guerra, P. L., & Nelson, S. W. (2011). Effective diversity facilitation matches teachers' cultural knowledge with the learning experience. *Journal of Staff Development, 32*(4), 73–74.

Gutiérrez, K. (2008). Developing a sociocritical literacy in the Third Space. *Reading Research Quarterly, 43*(2), 148–164.

Gutiérrez, K. D., Baquedano-López, P., & Tejeda, C. (2003). Rethinking diversity: Hybridity and hybrid language practices in the third space. In S. Goodman, T. Lillis, J. Maybin, & N. Mercer (Eds.), *Language, literacy, and education: A reader* (pp. 171–187). Trent, UK: The Open University.

Herrera, S. (2010). *Biography-driven culturally responsive teaching.* New York, NY: Teachers College Press.

Herrera, S. (2016). *Biography-driven culturally responsive teaching* (2nd ed.). New York, NY: Teachers College Press.

Herrera, S. G. (1995). *Junior high school teachers and the meaning perspectives they hold regarding their Mexican American students: An ethnographic case study* (Unpublished doctoral dissertation). Texas Tech University, Lubbock.

Herrera, S., Holmes, M., Murry, K., & Kavimandan, S. (2019). *Tipping the scales toward culturally responsive teaching: Teacher readiness for accommodative, biography-driven, instruction.* Paper presented at the annual meeting of AERA, Toronto, Canada.

Herrera, S., & Murry, K. (2005). *Mastering ESL and bilingual methods: Differentiated instruction for culturally and linguistically diverse (CLD) students.* Boston, MA: Pearson.

Herrera, S., & Murry, K. (2016). *Mastering ESL/EFL methods: Differentiated instruction for culturally and linguistically diverse (CLD) students* (3rd ed.). Boston: Pearson.

Herrera, S., Murry, K., & Holmes, M. (in press). The trajectory of the invisible teacher: Latinx teachers in search of professional belonging. In C. D. Gist & T. J. Bristol (Eds.), *Handbook of research on teachers of color.*

Hill, N. E., Witherspoon, D. P., & Bartz, D. (2018). Parental involvement in education during middle school: Perspectives of ethnically diverse parents, teachers, and students. *Journal of Educational Research, 111*(1), 12–27.

Howard, P. K. (2012, April 2). *To fix America's education bureaucracy, we need to destroy it.* Retrieved from www.theatlantic.com/national/archive/2012/04/to-fix-americas-education-bureaucracy-we-need-to-destroy-it/255173

Jerald, C. (n.d.). *School culture: The hidden curriculum.* Retrieved from www.readingrockets.org/article/school-culture-hidden-curriculum

Kressler, B., & Cavendish, W. (2019). High school teachers' sense-making of response to intervention: A critical practice analysis. *Education and Urban Society*, 1–26.

Lawson, M. (2003). School-family relations in context: Parent and teacher perceptions of parent involvement. *Urban Education, 38*(1), 77–133.

Liddicoat, A. J., Scarino, A., & Kohler, M. (2018). The impact of school structures and cultures on change in teaching and learning: The case of languages. *Curriculum Perspectives, 38*(3), 3–13.

Lightfoot, S. L. (1978). *Worlds apart: Relationships between families and schools.* New York, NY: Basic Books.

Lopez, G. (2001). The value of hard work: Lessons on parent involvement from an (im)migrant household. *Harvard Educational Review, 71*(3), 416–438. doi:10.17763/haer.71.3.43x7k542x023767u

Lopez, G. R., Scribner, J. D., & Mahitivanichch, K. (2001). Redefining parental involvement: Lessons from high-performing migrant-impacted schools. *American Educational Research Journal, 38*(2), 253–288.

Mendenhall, M., Bartlett, L., & Ghaffar-Kucher, A. (2017). If you need help, they are always there for us: Education for refugees in an international high school in New York City. *Urban Review, 49*(1), 1–25.

Mezirow, J. (2007). Adult education and empowerment for individual and community development. In B. Connolly, T. Fleming, D. McCormack, & A. Ryan (Eds.), *Radical learning for liberation* (pp. 10–17). Maynooth, Ireland: MACE.

Moje, E. B., Ciechanowsku, K. M., Kramer, K., Ellis, L., Carillo, R., & Collazo, T. (2004). Working toward third space in content area literacy: An examination of everyday funds of knowledge and discourse. *Reading Research Quarterly, 39*(1), 38–70.

Moll, L. C., & González, N. (2004). A funds-of-knowledge approach to multicultural education. In J. A. Banks & C. A. Banks (Eds.), *Handbook of research on multicultural education* (2nd ed., pp. 699–715). San Francisco, CA: Jossey Bass.

Morales, A., Abrica, E., & Herrera, S. (2019). The mañana complex: A revelatory narrative of teachers' White innocence and racial disgust toward Mexican-American children. *The Urban Review, 51*(3), 503–522.

Murry, K. (2012). Cognitive development, global learning, and academic progress: Promoting teacher readiness for CLD students and families. *Journal of Curriculum and Instruction, 6*(1), 11–24.

Nelson, S. W., & Guerra, P. L. (2014). Educator beliefs and cultural knowledge: Implications for school improvement efforts. *Educational Administration Quarterly, 50*(1), 67–95.

Nieto, S. (1992). *Affirming diversity: The sociopolitical context of multicultural education*. New York, NY: Longman.

Peck, C., & Reitzug, U. (2018). Discount stores, discount(ed) community? Parent and family engagement, community outreach, and an urban turnaround school. *Education and Urban Society, 50*(8), 675–696.

Souto-Manning, M., & Swick, K. (2006). Teachers' beliefs about parent and family involvement: Rethinking our family involvement paradigm. *Early Childhood Education Journal, 34*(2), 187–193.

Williams, T. T., & Sánchez, B. (2012). Parental involvement (and uninvolvement) at an inner-city high school. *Urban Education, 47*(3), 625–652.

CHAPTER 7

Furthering the Pedagogy of Hope

[M]y humanity is bound up in yours, for we can only be human together.

—Desmond Tutu, Archbishop (N. Tutu, 1989), p. 71

Key Concepts: aspirational assets, linguistic assets, familial assets, social assets, navigational assets, resistant assets

INTRODUCTION

The aim of this text is to speak to the heart of practitioners, leaders, and policymakers about ways to better reach and engage families, particularly those that are marginalized from the system. The fast-changing demographics of our schools urge the prioritization of this goal. Yet, to date, little has changed in the past 50 years regarding the ways we approach culturally and linguistically diverse (CLD) families. In order for this to occur, critical conversations and alternative perspectives must be explored.

In Chapter 6, the accommodation readiness spiral (ARS) sets the stage for critically reflecting on where you find yourself, as a professional, in readiness both to recognize the significance of currently marginalized families to the success of schools and to enhance your effectiveness as an educator in collaborating with and advocating for CLD students and their families. As illustrated by the ARS, that readiness is grounded in reflection that not only acknowledges assumptions in thinking (e.g., about CLD families) but also prompts reexamination of the validity of those assumptions. For example, some teachers find that CLD families do not come to their regularly scheduled parent–teacher conferences. A common assumption about these absent families is that they simply do not care about their children's education. However, family members often work night shifts, during which grandparents may care for their children. It would be unrealistic in this scenario to assume that CLD parents could attend after-school conferences for their children. Creating more realistic, responsive, meaningful opportunities for families to become engaged with the school requires teachers' creativity in rethinking family engagement.

The ARS also challenges us as educators to move beyond the espoused and *act*. To this end, we asked that you first audit your own thinking about families and students in order to move forward in meeting the needs of learners and recognizing the assets that each possesses. This chapter now moves the conversation from reflection to *hope, care*, and *love*. Hope opens the door for shifting our paradigms through activism and action. Care has the potential to reframe our perspectives from *feeling for, to feeling with*—a move toward empathy for caregivers and families that may not yet have the necessary skills to walk beside us on this journey we know as schooling. Love speaks to the humanity we attend to as we struggle to challenge outdated ways of thinking about parental involvement and shift paradigms as we blaze new pathways for attending to the needs, realities, and assets of our particular school or community.

In articulating this circle of hope, care, and love, we are reminded that we may think of hope as an anticipation of obtainment or fulfillment. On the one hand, this perspective enables us to act with the anticipation that doing so will enable us to obtain our goals. On the other hand, the perspective suggests that our action will not only benefit those for whom we act, but also fulfill our hearts and minds, as caring, loving, and humanistic professionals. In the sections that follow, we discuss ways the circle of hope, care, and love may be encouraged, acted upon, and facilitated at the levels of the district, school, and classroom.

THE DISTRICT

Our work in schools is often guided or mandated by school boards, central administration, and mantras that espouse (through vision and mission statements) what matters and should guide decisions for ensuring equitable schools for all. Think about the following sample of mission statements from school district websites:

- *Mission:* The mission of [school district name] is to work in partnership with students, families and the community to ensure that each student acquires the knowledge, skills, and core values necessary to achieve personal success and to enrich the community.
- *Mission:* The [school district name] graduates every student prepared for higher learning and careers to empower them as knowledgeable and engaged citizens, innovators, and drivers of a robust, bicultural economy.
- *Superintendent's Message:* At [school district name] our goal is to prepare students for the 21st century by engaging all learners in meaningful learning experiences that meet the highest educational and ethical standards in a caring, collaborative learning community supported through partnerships with parents and families, businesses, civic organizations, and higher education.

In our recent review of over 100 such mission statements across multiple states, only approximately 20% were found to incorporate the word *family.* For us, this finding prompted the following questions:

1. What exactly does it mean to be in partnership with the family?
2. In what ways do school boards and central office administrators draw on the knowledge and experiences of the community and families, irrespective of national origin, socioeconomic level, or language?
3. How has past and current legislation impacted the ways a district makes decisions that impact students and families?
4. What does central administration do for families and students? Do they even have a role?

A recent conversation with a group of central administrators offered few answers to such questions about families; it did confirm for us the difference between espoused notions of family partnerships and demonstrable actions in practice.

In reality, acting on district goals of family engagement is regularly left for school administrators to achieve. The silence on the appropriate role of central administration in forging an agenda that effectively actualizes a mission to involve marginalized families is almost deafening. In fact, a national study on the topic concluded that central offices of school districts offer schools and school leaders little encouragement to actively pursue family engagement, and even less guidance for the promotion and sustainment of such efforts (Aydin, 2011).

Despite these limitations, the language district leaders use *is* pivotal. Whether it is the prose of the district's mission statement or the language that central administrators use with school leaders and teachers, their guidance often drives the culture of the schools they oversee. If the infrastructures district leaders create, or the auditing criteria they follow, do not reflect support for family engagement, such engagement will not prove the asset to attainment of the district's mission that it should be.

It is beyond the scope of this book to address the sociopolitical realities that often are barriers to the promotion and maintenance of high levels of family engagement in district schools. Too often, the positionality of power and what is espoused fails to align with the reality experienced by families in the district. CLD family involvement in the schools often is left to *be managed* by Title I, Migrant, and Head Start program directors who are charged with attending to the needs of CLD families and their children in order to meet legislated requirements.

Advocacy is needed to push systems entrenched in unequal power dynamics to name inadequacies of guidance and support for the engagement of CLD and other marginalized families, petition for action that matches rhetoric, and offer hope for the future to students and their families. As caring, loving educators on the frontline, we hold the collective power to ask questions and drive a new agenda where action in the schools matches what is espoused in the visions and mission statements of school districts.

THE SCHOOL

Current school-centric models place the onus of parental involvement, engagement, or partnership on school leaders. Asked what parental involvement looks like in their schools, most administrators at this level report the use of familiar events designed for this purpose: family night, *cinco de mayo* celebration, book fair, trunk or treat, literacy and math nights, and other whole-school activities purportedly designed to get parents engaged in their children's education. By and large, this event-focused approach is an indicator of several points worth noting.

First, family is rarely the sole focus of the event. In turn, families may misinterpret the purpose of the event or conclude that family involvement was an afterthought. Second, such events often surround holidays or rites associated with just one cultural group. Families from other cultures may not interpret the event as open to, or designed for, them. Others may consider the focal holiday taboo. Third, such whole-school events are typically conducted after school and not attended by all school educators. Consequently, families may not understand that this is an opportunity for them to interact and plan with the teacher of their child. For those that do, the pertinent teacher may not be present on that night. Fourth, some CLD family members, especially those who have recently immigrated, may be intimidated by the notion of attending a whole-school event versus having a sit-down, one-on-one conversation with the teacher. For these and other reasons discussed throughout this text, attendance at such events may be low, and school administrators and teachers often lament the *lack of involvement* of the parents who do not attend. Culture-bound assumptions about students and families from another culture, especially those family members who do not speak English fluently, are among the most potent, persistent, and troublesome barriers to genuine family engagement.

The school itself tends to demonstrate its own culture as well, typically reflecting the values, perspectives, and beliefs of the educators who dominate its daily operation. Assumptions about CLD students and families may also influence PTA/PTO, site council, or party-planning committees at the school level. The outcomes of such deliberations often reflect a hegemonic view that limits the potential of what could be. What if this hegemonic discourse was disrupted? What if parent/family engagement were not about upcoming events or student achievement but, instead, were premised on building relationships that informed practice? What would happen if we *assumed* that learning about the CLD communities we serve could inform our curriculum and instruction? Think about the following questions:

1. In what ways does my perspective on family engagement go beyond programs and activities planned for the same time each year, year after year, to promote parent involvement?

2. Where does the school prioritize the experiences and funds of knowledge that families and caregivers bring (and could possibly share with the school)?
3. How does the school gather information in ways that communicate to families and caregivers that they are valuable contributors to the conversation?
4. Where do you fit into the conversation of family engagement at the school level?

New assumptions and new types of conversations require that we begin to ask atypical questions. For example, where do our school board, superintendent, and site-based principals stand in re-envisioning current paradigms toward creating more inclusive contexts for family engagement? Are they open to more compassionate, caring, and hopeful ways of connecting with families, listening to their perspectives, and maximizing their assets whenever they may be able to contribute to teaching and learning within our schools? If not, in what ways and with what evidence can we advocate for more open, loving, and proactive efforts to maximize genuine family engagement—efforts likely to increase achievement, reduce absences and referrals, and give the community a greater stake in the success of the school? A context of trust, compassion, and authentic relationships that minimize assumptions and prejudgments through critical reflection will be pivotal to our success. In such a context, we are in the best position to move forward collaboratively.

At the *collective* school level, consider how teachers' first point of contact with each parent/caregiver could inform the larger school community. A colleague once shared that after a migrant parent meeting, she had asked one parent, "What would you want us to do as a school to support you?" The response was, *"Nada más que la gente, me trate con respeto y me salude"* (Just that everyone treats me with respect and says hello to me). The culture of the school speaks volumes as to how families will engage.

Often teachers feel sadness for students when their parents do not volunteer or participate in the yearly school carnival. Questions to ask ourselves at such moments include: Is the school carnival the most appropriate activity for the community being served? Are there other school-based activities that could be envisioned and planned more organically, using what teachers learn from students and families about their biographies, daily routines/obligations, and beliefs about education? Sometimes, the best first step is to begin asking what caregivers want, expect, bring, need, and cherish.

At the school level, teachers often are in the most favorable position to begin re-imagining parent/caregiver/family engagement. Disrupting what has been will require building new relationships through phone calls, active listening during instruction, and harvesting of social and cultural capital from the community to plan more inclusive, better attended, and distinctly intentional opportunities for caregivers to contribute their capital to the goals of the school.

THE CLASSROOM

When we think about classrooms, we remember that students are at the heart of all our efforts. Consider the following student reflection:

> I knew my teacher cared. She knew my floors were bare and cold in the winter. She knew that money was scarce in my home. She knew my parents worked from sun up to sun down just to pay the rent and feed us. I knew she cared when she gave me 30 colorful pieces of carpet to place upon the bare floors in the room in which we slept, rolled in blankets to keep warm. With warmth in her eyes, a light of happiness and care, she unloaded the pieces and praised my mother for her skill in sewing. She knew, from what I had shared at school, that my mother was gifted with the old sewing machine that she still used and loved.
>
> She spoke in English, a big smile on her lips. She knew my mother would not understand beyond the glow of her face. I felt proud and translated her warm and genuine way of being a teacher who looked beyond my struggles. She praised my father for his hard work in teaching us to respect others. Ms. Coggin cared. She cared so much that she knew my parents' struggles and respected them for who they were without judgment for the many absences. I played an adult role in my home. She understood. No blame, no shame, just care, love, and hope.

The classroom teacher is one of the most powerful influencers for family engagement that is grounded in culturally responsive, relationship-bound ways of fostering and nurturing a place of hope, both for the family and the learner. No individual in the daily interactions of the CLD family is more pivotal in her or his capacity to engage the caregiver in a pedagogy of hope than the *teacher*—the person who shares the daily responsibility of unfolding all of life's possibilities for the child.

Not all children arrive in our classrooms with the same biopsychosocial history (Aydin, 2011; Herrera, 2016). However, most arrive with a deep, inner desire to learn and grow. Life circumstances are the hand of cards dealt to each of us. For children and their families, there are often numerous obstacles without many choices. Yet children begin the journey again every time we open the door with care and love and provide the space to have hope for a better future. It's a journey that begins and ends, one day at a time.

As authors, we recognize the need for parental engagement frameworks and models to draw initial parameters for school activities. After all, a playbook is always important to ensure something takes place. However, we also envision that what you have read in this book will move you to rewrite your own narrative based on the learners you serve, year to year. Their stories will change, and your position within each family will be defined by the ways you build a relationship uniquely derived from what is learned.

In her work on the ethics of care, Nel Noddings (1984) examined components of authentic caring. She reminded us that well-intended actions may not always lead to positive outcomes for those for whom we are caring. This especially holds true when the act of caring is entered into, long before the caregiver (e.g., the teacher) gets to know the person receiving the care. For families and educators, building a relationship is like a courtship. We must remember that, on both sides, walls of fear, oppression, and hegemony took years to become part of our way of viewing and experiencing interactions. Caring, loving, and hopeful relationships take just as long to build.

Noddings reminds us that disconnects between families and schools often occur without school officials understanding why. In part, this is so because organizational styles in schools tend to favor a cookie-cutter approach to families, wherein each family receives similar treatment, even if their needs or desires may differ. Noddings (1984) has argued that a superior goal is to build on natural caring (an individual's inclination to care) to create an ethic of caring reliant on our belief that caring is the appropriate way of building relationships with one another. When this is the goal, a cycle of caring between individuals begins and, if those involved are persistent, a culture of caring is possible.

Noddings has correlated the notion of care with valuing the whole child. She has written,

> We will not find the solution to problems of violence, alienation, ignorance, and unhappiness in increasing our security, imposing more tests, punishing schools for their failure to produce 100 percent proficiency, or demanding that teachers be knowledgeable in the subjects they teach. Instead, we must allow teachers and students to interact as whole persons, and we must develop policies that treat the school as a whole community. (2005, p. 13)

Through caring interactions and communication, a teacher gathers the necessary tools to engage with the parent/caregiver from a place of understanding and respect, where judgment of the other is left outside the door.

Creating partnerships and engaging with parents/caregivers are emotional acts. Such acts are not always comfortable or well reciprocated, but they open spaces to learn about similarities and work through differences. Engagement requires time and energy by all parties. Educators hold the key to letting go of the many deficit perspectives that have made schools dysfunctional, inequitable spaces for CLD and other students for decades (Ladson-Billings & Tate, 1995). A future of caring must move us toward understanding that wealth or *capital* is not always best measured by one's educational level or bank account. Instead, wealth is often found within the cultural, linguistic, cognitive, and sociocultural lived experiences that a person has amassed though years of social, educational, and professional interactions.

Letting go of positions of power and creating equitable spaces that focus on what is best for the learner will prove challenging for many of us, as educators. In these mutually negotiated spaces, both the parent/caregiver and teacher become equals, and the creation of something new and synergistic becomes a palpable possibility (Lasky, 2001; Smit, Driessen, Sleegers, & Teelken, 2008). Nevertheless, the full potential of these mutual efforts to improve outcomes will become reality only when the potential for mistrust between parents/ caregivers and teachers is acknowledged, regularly reflected on, and addressed equitably.

Imagine what would be possible if, through ongoing conversations, activities were decided from a grassroots agenda. Early in the school year, teachers could come together to talk about the knowledge bases and experiential backgrounds that caregivers/families could bring to their classrooms. Teachers could then maximize family members' biographies of knowledge, skills, and capacities in creative ways to enrich the curriculum, engage students with instruction, and enhance caregivers' dispositions toward engagement with the teacher and the school. Take time to *imagine the possibilities for your classroom,* your school, your community of caring for each other, and sharing hope for a brighter tomorrow.

DEFINING CAPITAL THROUGH AN ASSET-BASED PERSPECTIVE

Yosso (2005) identified six possible sources of capital to draw on when learning from students and their families: aspirational, linguistic, familial, social, navigational, and resistant capital. Recognizing critical perspectives on the word *capital,* we authors choose to reframe the word to characterize the many *assets* that caregivers/families contribute to education. Yosso's work has set the stage to move critical reflection on what we *espouse* to be in pursuit of for students and families, into actions for disrupting and dismantling deficit ways of thinking and doing to build genuine relationships with caregivers/families. Following are practical ideas for reframing our thinking within classroom practice to draw on untapped resources from the community and families.

1. ***Aspirational assets:*** Every family has high hopes for the students they care for every day. Life does not always provide the opportunity to showcase it in "typical" ways. We must create opportunities to document what the aspirations were/are for the family, and where they see the learner fitting in. What are the challenges to achieving their hopes and dreams? We all have dreams; sometimes they play out differently than expected.
2. ***Linguistic assets:*** Families and students generally come to us ready to learn a second language. Bilingualism/multilingualism is an asset often overlooked by educators. Capital in the form of songs, poetry, *dichos* (sayings), and *cuentos* (stories) is frequently left out of the classroom. Often these assets are easily transferred into English. We educators

often perceive lack of proficiency in English, as such a deficit that we cannot begin to teach until the learner is proficient, based on our own assessment. We encourage teachers to gather from the parent/caregiver or other family member artifacts that are found in the native language that will make the family present within the classroom. We all have stories, music, poetry, and more. Take time and you will see there is more to literacy and language than speaking English.

3. *Familial assets:* Family is where our story begins. Often family refers to those related to us by blood; however, family also encompasses those in our life who care for our needs. Those individuals fill in for us when our parents/caregivers cannot. Family is much more than just our parents. Seek out those caring adults that learners identify as part of their extended families—the adults with whom they have built a trusting, loving relationship. Reach out for the people who can be present to mediate learning and engagement when the challenges parents face hinder their ability to respond to what we need.

4. *Social assets:* Over time, the learner identifies those individuals who have become part of an unspoken network that provides support. This network might include the paraprofessional who lives down the street, the former teacher who will step in to represent, the neighbor who is always willing to be there, in whatever ways, whenever needed. Find and document the learner's allies. Social assets support and encourage CLD learners to the finish line.

5. *Navigational assets:* For some students, getting to school and our classrooms each day requires that at a very early age they learn to navigate the tense world that society creates. Inherent to many spaces is the balance of living simultaneously in two worlds with often opposing sets of rules and language. CLD families and students learn to read cues in ways that require cognitive functions that white, native-English speakers may never use. Draw on these navigational assets and celebrate a family's ability to navigate two very different spaces.

6. *Resistant assets:* Seek to recognize the distance parents/caregivers and students may initially have toward engagement in the classroom. What experiences have they had in the past? What is the history that may be causing the parent/caregiver

to resist (often self-defensively) becoming part of the fabric of the classroom or school community? Work to create a truly safe space for CLD students and families in your classroom. By demonstrating unflinching respect, care, and valuing of student/family assets, despite the passage of time, you increase the likelihood that families will recognize your authenticity and begin to trust. They will begin to see you as an ally in the struggle for greater equity and justice in their own lives and in the larger society.

Re-envisioning for the future will require learning from parents/caregivers/families, and communities. This will only be possible if, as leaders and educators, we intentionally identify assets and let go of normative ideas about engagement and ways of being an involved parent.

LOVE AND HOPE:
ONE QUESTION AND STEP AT A TIME

In our work as teachers, we do not judge; rather, we look for the good in every parent. Consider the following student reflection:

My parents were not like all parents. They never made it to school in the years since I arrived from Mexico. There were more important things to take care of: working, taking care of the house, and surviving. I thank my teacher for telling me often how lucky I was to have parents who worked so hard, for understanding they could not help me with homework because not only was there no time, they didn't speak the language. They didn't have the resources. My teacher knew to praise my parents for what they could do. She never drew the lines for who they were supposed to be. She taught me that they loved me. She showed me that there was hope. She reminded me that through their hard work, they imagined a different world for me. Her words were the unspoken words my parent carried in their minds. Their hopes and dreams were translated by the teacher who knew ALL parents hope and dream for their children. She walked beside me and carried me through her words, reminding me how amazing my family was. What assets they had were instilled in me: persistence, passion, humility, work ethic, compassion, and love.

As previously discussed, our intention as authors was not to create a new model for parental engagement. Innovative strategies already exist for enhancing parent/caregiver communication, inclusive curricula, and school- and districtwide family engagement initiatives. Rather, our hope is to encourage and promote a *critical consciousness* for our collective thinking, questioning, and planning for family engagement. Doing so begins with giving credence to families.

Family engagement is often limited in scope and seen as a means to an end. In other words, motives for including the family are often driven by the desire to improve student outcomes, boost attendance at school functions, and/or seek assistance with classroom duties and fundraising events. For some in the field, this is enough reason to pursue family engagement. We disagree with this sentiment and believe we have yet to embrace the essence of family and community engagement.

Public schools are institutions that operate systematically with little change. Innovative ideas can be found throughout classrooms and communities, but the system itself relies on fossilized practices that often thwart intercultural understanding and healthy communities. These dynamics are apparent in classrooms, too, as we continue to assign the same homework packets and teach the same lesson on family trees 5 decades later. Why are we continually doing the same things year after year? As discussed, we are prone to follow the path of least resistance, especially when it is to our benefit. After all, it is familiar and comfortable, and we feel confident and secure doing things as they have always been done. Yet who is responsible for speaking up when these procedures are no longer effective?

The reality is that the demographics of this country are changing and will continue to change. Some see this fact as a threat to the fabric of American ideals while others welcome the idea of multiple languages, identities, and cultures woven into the tapestry of what this nation represents. Either way, fossilized practices in leading, teaching, and collaborating with families continue to exist. As a result, we are not reaching, supporting, validating, or engaging the majority of families represented in U.S. schools today. It is time to begin the process of humbly unlearning.

We argue that the dynamics of fostering reciprocal relationships and authentic *cariño* with families is much more complex than simply defining a role and fossilizing its duties. In the classroom, educators tend to have a creative spirit that seeks to find whatever works to enhance results. Why are we so hesitant to have this same approach in growing relations with families? Families are not peripheral to the happenings of the school. They are the primary socializing agents of the children in our schools, and they serve as our partners in helping students feel loved, supported, and safe in their pursuit of learning and discovery.

Schools are more than buildings, and communities are more than geographic locales. They are about the people that share space as they navigate the challenges and celebrate the joys this world brings. We must not hide behind our roles or let our daily duties insulate us from wanting or needing to look beyond traditions.

We must recognize our own cultural capital and racial privilege and explore how these influence our ways of being and seeing. Numerous times, we have heard educators state that teaching is not political, and that to begin advocating for systemic social change would only place them in danger of losing their jobs. We empathize with these very real sentiments. However, quoting Thomas Mann, German novelist, social critic, and Nobel Prize recipient of literature, "Everything is politics." Public education and the profession of teaching are extremely political, from the subject matter taught, to the allocation of funding, to the stark reality that the demographics of today's teachers do not match those of their students.

After spending years of training on contextualization in teacher education courses and curricula, why are we still unable to realize that without incorporating family narratives as well as societal issues into our teaching and schoolwide initiatives, we will continue to uphold practices that reinforce hegemonic views and marginalize CLD families? This is not about deciding what families need in order to "fix" their circumstances, or viewing students and parents/caregivers from a *"pobrecito"* perspective. Instead, making changes requires honest and critical reflection. In what ways do we spend time engaging and reaching out, instead of fruitlessly attempting to pull families in? Asking families to comply with predetermined notions of what family and engagement should look like only further solidifies us/them mentalities. Such distinctions reinforce entrenched stereotypes that then necessitate conversations surrounding equity. Have we spent time reflecting on the bias within our schools and within ourselves? Have we "unpacked our knapsacks," as Peggy McIntosh (1989) asks? If not, why?

We can create new terms, develop new models, and purchase multiple social media platforms and apps for our school's families. However, such efforts should not be our starting place for parental engagement. The core ingredients, from a humanistic perspective (which likely drew us to the field of education in the first place), are *relationships*. Our relationships with families, however, must be defined by honesty, respect, and love. Part of transforming the parent engagement triad begins with our stepping aside and allowing families and community members to actively create spaces to foster relations. We are not naïve in thinking that advocating for the coexistence of multiple voices, agendas, and happenings can sometimes cause tensions. However, difference brings endless possibilities when establishing a social network energized by and committed to the lives of children.

CONCLUSION

Humanity is in need of love. The world is full of stresses, conflict, and tragedy. Our students come to school carrying these realities, and our families are doing their best to navigate each passing day. How can we begin to bring authentic *cariño* to the concept of family engagement? Above all, the motive, purpose, and outcome of family engagement should focus on how people are treated. Radical kinship begins when we honor the multiple ways family is defined, the endless contributions families offer, the equal role of each member of the engagement triad, and the belief that unity through diversity is possible.

The pictures in Figure 7.1 remind us that no single picture of family exists. Love and hope are possible when we leave the canvas open to be defined by the parents/caregivers/families we serve. As educators, our voices have the potential to inform. Collectively, *we can* advocate for letting go of school-centric ways of thinking and doing. Every family and child deserve to be celebrated for who they are and what they bring to this space we call school. As this book's title suggests, when we begin the process of humbly unlearning, equitable spaces for family engagement with schools emerge. Let us work together to push boundaries, create pathways, and open doors to new possibilities.

Figure 7.1. Trees, Leaves, Flowers, and Houses: Symbols of Family Kinship

Guatemalan Tree

Mexican Leaves

Mexican Flowers

Somali House

Source: Linn Elementary, Dodge City, Kansas

Check It Out
(Questions to Guide Reflection and Discussion)

1. As you consider what you read in Chapter 7, do the following:
   • Read the poem, "Unity," below.
   • Reflect on the students you serve. What "clay" are you molding in your teaching and learning space?

Plan It Out
(Creating an Idea That Requires Action)

2. In a team, think and act on the following:
   • Identify the assets each of the parents/caregivers/families you serve brings to the teaching context.

Try It Out
(Attempting Action and Reflecting upon Outcomes)

3. Create your action plan:
   • Develop action steps for yourself for next week.
   • Chart out your overarching plans for the remainder of the month and year.
   • Along your journey, stop periodically to assess your own growth as well as the status of your relationships with students and families.
   • Document lessons learned and make notes of changes you will make for the future.

Unity

I dreamt I stood in a studio,
And watched two sculptors there.
The clay they used was a young child's mind,
And they fashioned it with care.

One was a teacher—the tools she used,
Were books, music, and art.
The other, a parent—working with a guiding hand,
And a gentle loving heart.

Day after day, the teacher toiled
With a touch that was deft and sure.
While the parent labored by her side,
And polished and smoothed it o'er.

And when at last, their task was done,
They were proud of what they had wrought.
For the things they had molded into the child,
Could neither be sold nor bought.

And each agreed they would have failed
If each had worked alone,
For behind the teacher stood the school,
And behind the parent, the home.

—Author Unknown

REFERENCES

Aydin, N. G. (2011). *A national study: School counselor involvement in school, family and community partnerships with linguistically diverse families* (Unpublished doctoral dissertation). University of Iowa, Iowa City. Retrieved from ir .uiowa.edu/cgi/viewcontent.cgi?article=3255&context=etd

Herrera, S. (2016). *Biography-driven culturally responsive teaching* (2nd ed.). New York, NY: Teachers College Press.

Ladson-Billings, G., & Tate, W. F., IV (1995). Toward a critical race theory of education. *Teachers College Record, 97*(1), 47–68.

Lasky, S. (2001). The cultural and emotional politics of teacher-parent interactions. *Teaching and Teacher Education, 17*(4), 403–425.

McIntosh, P. (1989, July/August). White privilege: Unpacking the invisible knapsack. *Peace and Freedom Magazine,* 10–12.

Noddings, N. (1984). *Caring: A feminine approach to ethics and moral education.* Berkeley and Los Angeles: University of California Press.

Noddings, N. (2005). *Educating citizens for global awareness.* New York, NY: Teachers College Press.

Smit, F., Driessen, G., Sleegers, P., & Teelken, C. (2008). Scrutinizing the balance: Parental care versus educational responsibilities in a changing society. *Early Child Development and Care, 178*(1), 65–80.

Tutu, N. (1989). *The words of Desmond Tutu.* New York, NY: New Market Press.

Yosso, T. J. (2005). Whose culture has capital? A critical race theory discussion of community cultural wealth. *Race Ethnicity and Education, 8*(1), 69–91.

Index

Note: Page numbers followed by "*f*" and "*t*" indicate figures and tables respectively.

About the Authors

Dr. Socorro Herrera is a professor in the Department of Curriculum and Instruction, College of Education at Kansas State University and the executive director of the Center for Intercultural and Multilingual Advocacy (CIMA). As an international keynote speaker, district consultant, and trainer of trainers, she has collaborated with families, teachers, and administrators in charting new paths for the success of culturally and linguistically diverse students. Her research focuses on literacy and academic opportunities with students and their families, reading strategies, and preservice and in-service teacher preparation. She is the best-selling author of *Biography-Driven Culturally Responsive Teaching.*

Dr. Lisa Porter is an assistant professor of sociology at James Madison University in Harrisonburg, Virginia. She began her teaching as a SDAIE high school content teacher in migrant education in southern California before transitioning to adult education as an ESL teacher serving immigrant and refugee families in Massachusetts. She has taught in multiple countries with students of all ages prior to settling in Virginia. Currently, she serves as an associate editor for the *Journal of Interdisciplinary Studies in Education* and co-chairs the Many Voices of Harrisonburg, a community-based collaborative dedicated to enhancing community relations. Her scholarly work within the sociology of education focuses on equitable relationships between families, schools, and communities.

Dr. Katherine Barko-Alva is an assistant professor and director of the ESL/Bilingual Education program at William & Mary, School of Education, in Williamsburg, Virginia. Katherine Barko-Alva, a former McKnight fellow at the University of Florida, holds a PhD in curriculum and instruction in the area of ESL/bilingual education. As an award-wining scholar, her research agenda focuses on how DLBE/ESL educators make sense of language in culturally and linguistically diverse K–12 contexts. With more than 14 years of professional experience teaching as well as designing and implementing job-embedded professional development practices at the national and international level, her lived experiences as an English learner in a U.S. school guide the nature of her work and commitment to families, teachers, and students.